THE BATTLE FOR THE ATLANTIC

THE BATTLE
FOR THE
ATLANTIC

Jay Williams

Maps by Richard Edes Harrison

RANDOM HOUSE · NEW YORK

Grateful acknowledgment is made to the following for permission to quote copyrighted material from the sources specified:

To Houghton Mifflin Company, publishers of *The Grand Alliance* by Winston Churchill; to the National Maritime Union of America, AFL-CIO, publishers of *The Pilot;* to Little, Brown & Company and the Atlantic Monthly Press, publishers of *The Battle of the Atlantic, 1939-1943,* by Samnel Eliot Morison; to Rinehart and Company, publishers of *North Atlantic Patrol: The Log of a Seagoing Artist* (1943), by Griffith Baily Coale, USNR.

SECOND PRINTING

© Copyright, 1959, by Jay Williams
All rights reserved under International and Pan-American Copyright Conventions. Published in New York by Random House, Inc., and simultaneously in Toronto, Canada, by Random House of Canada, Limited. Library of Congress Catalog Card Number: 59-5520
Manufactured in the United States of America
by H. Wolff, New York

Author's Note

I wish to thank the Office of Information, Department of the Navy, and the National Maritime Union for their co-operation and assistance. I am grateful, also, to Rear Admiral Paul R. Heineman for his permission to use material relating to him, and for his kindness in sending me much information. Material relating to the naval career of Commander Frederic Walker was drawn from, among other sources, the books *Walker, RN,* by Terence Robertson, Evans Brothers, London, 1956, and *Walker's Groups in the Western Approaches,* by D. E. G. Wemyss, Liverpool *Daily Post and Echo,* Liverpool, 1948.

I am indebted for brilliant insights into the geographical problems involved to the work of the cartographer, Richard Edes Harrison, and for many specific details and much information to the great and exhaustive work, *History of United States Naval Operations in World War II,* by Samuel Eliot Morison.

—JAY WILLIAMS

Contents

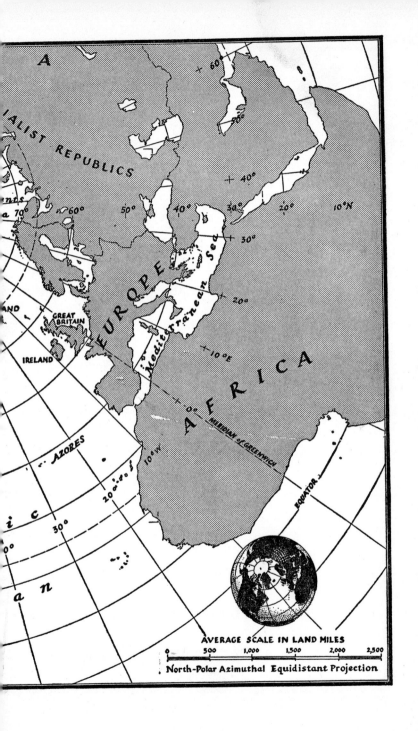

AVERAGE SCALE IN LAND MILES

0   500   1,000   1,500   2,000   2,500

North-Polar Azimuthal Equidistant Projection

THE BATTLE FOR THE ATLANTIC

1

The Battle with No Foxholes

You might say that the Battle of the Atlantic began on a moonless night at the end of May, 1940, in the little seaport town of Dunkirk, in Northern France. The British Expeditionary Force, which had landed so confidently to face the Germans only a short time before, was now driven back by a strong Nazi advance. They retreated to Dunkirk where they were hemmed in on every side by the enemy. While French units fought a savage rear-guard action to hold back the Germans, preparations were made for saving as many of the troops as possible, by sea.

A fleet set out from England. It was composed of everything that would float: destroyers, transport vessels, fishing craft, tugboats, private sailboats, even ferryboats. The pilots were not only regular navy men and merchant seamen, but civilians of all sorts—men, women, and even children.

Staff officers believed that no more than a small number of the troops—perhaps thirty or forty thousand—could be brought off safely. But on a calm sea, in swirls of fog, the hundreds of boats moved in. They were protected by every available airplane that could be sent up. The German fliers were knocked out of the air. Within the week, more than 330,000 men were carried back to England.

It was one of the most amazing retreats in history. Although it marked a defeat, it was a victory as well. Most of the British Expeditionary Force, as well as some French, Belgian, and other troops, were saved. But they had left their equipment behind. They had no tanks, no heavy guns, and almost no ammunition. The British planes were excellent, but they could not be built as rapidly as they were needed. There were far fewer of them than there were of the German aircraft.

From this moment on, Britain stood alone and almost helpless against the greatest army the world had ever seen. Within a month, Italy had entered the war on the side of the Germans, France had surrendered, and the Nazis prepared to smash England.

Germany's first aim was to beat the English to their knees by systematic heavy bombing. To begin with, a hundred bombers a day were sent over the cities, then two hundred, then nearly a thousand every single day. At the same time, the Germans hoped to close a ring of submarines and surface ships around the little island, so that all supplies would be cut off. When the English were starved and cowed, the Germans would then invade and destroy them.

But several things prevented this from happening as planned.

In the first place, while Germany was taking over France, the British had a breathing space in which to prepare themselves. They built up their defenses and began to make tanks and planes. War factories went full blast, and the workday ran fifteen or sixteen hours. There was no thought in anyone's mind of relaxing.

Second, although America was still not involved in the war, her leaders saw clearly that England must be helped. Munitions, weapons, food and clothing, ships and manufactured goods of all sorts were sent across the sea. There was only one good route, that by way of the North Atlantic. England was like a castle under siege, with one dangerous little back gate through which supplies could be smuggled. But the supplies came in.

Another item on which the Germans had not

counted at all was that the British people refused to be beaten to their knees. In spite of daily bombings, in spite of the deaths of thousands of civilians, the British went grimly on about their business. Night after night the bombs fell on homes and factories. Streets turned into piles of brick and stone and charred wood. The subway stations were full of sleeping people, sheltering there from the air raids. Men went to work in the morning without knowing whether they'd find their homes and families still there in the evening, and yet they continued to go to work. The factories still smoked. The tanks and guns and planes came off the assembly lines. And the British dug in tighter than before.

And lastly, Britain had a new prime minister who was to lead the country through all the years of war to ultimate victory. He was Winston Churchill, who took office in May, 1940.

He had been First Lord of the Admiralty. He referred to himself in some of his letters as "Former Naval Person." And he was thus better fitted than anyone else, perhaps, to see that a battle must be fought—and won—for the control of the seas.

"Battles might be won or lost," he said, "enterprises might succeed or miscarry, territories might be gained or quitted, but dominating all our power to carry on the war or even keep ourselves alive, lay our mastery of the ocean routes and the free approach and entry to our ports."

Britain was an island. She needed planes, tanks, guns, and ships. She needed food and ammunition and tools. Without all these, she was like a man on a mountaintop trying to fight with only his bare hands a forest fire creeping up on all sides. The countries of Europe were closed to her. She had to turn to the other nations of the Commonwealth—Australia, South Africa, Canada. But above all, she had to turn to the richest country in the world, and one which was still neutral: the United States.

Britain had bought millions of dollars' worth of food and weapons, and paid for them. But now she could no longer pay. It was at this point that President Franklin D. Roosevelt proposed the principle of Lend-Lease. By this principle, England would receive some supplies on long-term loans and would borrow weapons.

President Roosevelt said, "Suppose my neighbor's house catches fire and I have a length of garden hose four or five hundred feet away. If he can take my garden hose and connect it up with his hydrant, I may help him put out the fire. Now . . . I don't say to him before that operation, 'Neighbor, my hose cost me fifteen dollars; you have to pay me fifteen dollars for it.' No! . . . I don't want fifteen dollars—I want my garden hose back after the fire is over."

But the garden hose had to be brought to England's hydrant. The convoys of ships were attacked by long-range airplanes based in Europe, by submarines, by huge battleships and cruisers, and by magnetic mines that were drawn to the turning motors of ships and thus blew them up. Millions of tons of shipping went to the bottom. It became clear that it was not enough just to bring ships through safely. The test of survival depended on landing huge masses of equipment and supplies in England.

In 1941 the Germans were turning out submarines at the rate of ten a month. In only three months of that year, the dozen or so submarines operating continuously in the North Atlantic sank 142 ships. Earlier that same year two German battle cruisers, *Scharnhorst* and *Gneisenau,* in a two-month raid sank 22 ships, amounting to 115,000 tons.

The German High Command said gleefully, "In the spring our U-boat war will begin at sea . . . the air force will play its part, and the entire armed forces will bring a decision by hook or by crook."

It was clear to Mr. Churchill that the war must be made a long one, until the Germans weakened and perhaps other great countries could be drawn in on England's side. But every day more and more ships went down, fewer goods came through, and the chances of surviving were slimmer.

One day in March, 1941, the report of sinkings was brought to the War Cabinet by Admiral of the Fleet Sir Dudley Pound. Mr. Churchill had already seen them; the losses that week were exceptionally heavy. He said to Admiral Pound, "We have got to lift this business to the highest plane, over everything else. I am going to proclaim 'the Battle of the Atlantic.'"

Within a very few days, a committee was formed. It was named the Battle of the Atlantic Committee, and its task was to solve the most pressing problems: how to beat the long-range German bombers and the submarines, how to build new ships, how to fight back and see to it that England received the materials she needed so badly to carry on the war.

This was the official beginning of the fight that had begun the year before. Its climax was to come three years later, when the ocean was clear enough to enable the Allies to mass sufficient men, ships, and equipment to invade the coast of Normandy, on D-Day. Like all the other battles in the war this one was fought in the air

11

and on the surface. But unlike the others, it had another dimension: under the water. And the fighters rarely saw each other, except as blurred images in a periscope or dots of light on a screen. It was a battle in which there were no foxholes —no place for the fighters to hide.

In this strange battle, a few men could kill a thousand with one relatively light blow. Or a ship dropping thousands of tons of explosives might never know whether the enemy had been hurt or not. Gains and losses were rarely measured by the number of men killed, and never by any territory taken. Instead, they were measured by tons of shipping and cargo. Above all, as we shall see, it was from the very beginning a battle in which appearances were deceiving.

2

The Road across the Sea

World War II was often called a global war. It embraced the entire globe of the earth, taking in places with strange names that few were familiar with: Iwo Jima, Anzio, Murmansk, and El Alamein. But many people still could not get it through their heads that the earth *was* a globe. Although it was round, they had always seen it in flat maps.

The maps most of us know best are called Mercator projections. They are so named for their first maker, Gerardus Mercator, who published them in 1568. They show true compass directions and the true shapes of land masses, and they were developed for the use of sailing-ship captains. But they are exact only along the equator: they do not show the earth as it really is. People who are used to looking at Mercator's projections, with north at the top of the map and everything distorted above and below the equator, are greatly surprised when they learn that ninety-three percent of the world's people and three-quarters of the world's habitable land are located in the north latitudes. They are surprised to find that the only European capitals south of Washington, D.C., are Athens and Lisbon. And Venice, in Italy, which is thought of as a sunny southern city, is actually 150 miles farther north than the Siberian port of Vladivostok.

Consequently, when the war began, few people realized that the real center of our world was the north polar sea. If you could sail high above the earth in a space ship, and look down upon it from above the North Pole, you would see that all the continents except Australia and the frozen Antarctic form a great land mass around this polar sea. You would see clearly that North America, instead of looking like an island separated from the rest of the world by two oceans, is part of that mass. And Alaska, instead of being a distant outpost in the wilderness, is a natural jumping-off place for all the shortest air routes from the United States to Asia. Also, you would see that the little island of Iceland and the tip of Greenland, instead of being far outside the lines of travel, are stepping stones on the shortest route from America to England.

It was lucky, to begin with, that the leaders of the Allied Nations looked at the world this way, for it was to prove one of the most important views of the war. The Germans saw it too —some of them, at any rate—for one of their military experts wrote, "Whoever possesses Iceland holds a pistol firmly pointed at England,

America, and Canada." The question was, who would seize the pistol first.

Very early in the war, the Nazis marched into Norway and Denmark. In a matter of days, official resistance had ended and the Germans were firmly entrenched. The strategic countries of Iceland and Greenland were both Danish possessions. Accordingly, in May of 1940, England was invited by the government of Iceland to send troops into that country to protect it against a possible German invasion. At almost the same time, the local government of Greenland asked for American protection. This was given unofficially, two months later. The first steps were thus taken to protect the sea road.

England needed food, weapons and ammunition, iron and steel, and timber. Above all, she needed ships in which to carry all these things. Some of this material could come from Canada, but most of it had to come from the United States. A series of secret discussions was held, first in England, later in America. There was some confusion in the beginning over differences in the words the two countries used: for example, the British staff prepared a report which they felt was very urgent. They wanted to bring it up for discussion, so they said they "wanted to table it." To the Americans, tabling it meant putting off any discussion about it. There was a long, hot argument until both sides discovered they really wanted the same thing—to discuss the matter at once. However, aside from such complications, one simple fact was clear. Britain was determined to hold out against the Nazis, and was showing that she could do so. On this basis she required—and got—as much help as the United States could give at that time.

A very important deal was made between the two countries. In exchange for fifty old destroyers, England gave the United States the right to establish naval, military, and air bases in a number of British islands in the Western Hemisphere: Jamaica, Trinidad, St. Lucia, Antigua, Guiana, and the Bahamas. Later in the war, these bases were to prove extremely valuable in the fight against the U-boats in the Caribbean

Sea. On the same day the Germans began their air attack on London, British naval crews took over the first eight American destroyers, at Halifax.

The ocean route for supplies was now a series of stepping stones along what is called a Great Circle. Although people used the phrase "as the crow flies" for centuries, it never became a practical reality until the development of the airplane. The Great Circles are primarily air routes, distances between places "as the crow flies"—that is, the shortest way between two points on the earth's surface. With few exceptions, these show as curved lines on a Mercator projection. To see them as straight lines, you must either look at a globe of the world or at a special type of flat map called a gnomonic projection. The Great Circle route between Canada and England passes close to Newfoundland, Greenland, and Iceland. These are the stepping stones.

From these points, escort ships could travel with the convoys as protection against attack by submarines, and airplanes could fly out to give cover and to search for U-boats. American supplies were sent to Halifax, and then escorted by Canadian ships to a meeting place in mid-ocean where British escorts took over and guarded them the rest of the way.

The security of Greenland was essentially America's problem. On the icy east coast, the Germans had a weather station which sent regular reports to U-boats operating in northern waters. More disturbing, word came that they planned to base an air squadron on that coast. If this happened, not only ships but cities would be in constant danger.

The United States Coast Guard, which had always been prepared to do a little of everything, was sent to survey the Greenland coast. It was not until 1941, however, that Denmark and the United States signed an agreement by which America became the official protector of Greenland, and the Greenland Patrol was formed. This patrol was under the command of "Iceberg" Smith—Commander Edward H. Smith, who was one of the world's leading experts on ice and an authority on oceanography. His duties were wide and numerous, typical of the Coast Guard's readiness to do anything. They included convoying United States Army transports and supply ships, ice-breaking, the destruction of enemy radio or weather stations in Greenland, surveys, communications, air-sea rescue missions, and the stationing of weather-reporting ships.

At about the same time, Britain established escort and air bases in Iceland. This meant that her surface escort ships could move farther westward to protect merchant vessels. But the Germans sent their submarines farther west, too, and the slaughter increased. One convoy after another out of Halifax was attacked; in one month, twenty ships out of a convoy of thirty-four were sunk, and in one week twenty-seven ships were sent to the bottom, many from a single convoy.

Although the U-boats were the greatest menace, there were others almost as important. The Commander in Chief of the German fleet, Admiral Raeder, was an accomplished naval officer, and even though he constantly had to oppose his own leader, Hitler, who knew and cared little for sea war, he was able to make things extremely hot for the British. He fitted out a number of merchant ships as raiders, fast, well armed, and with small airplanes for reconnaissance. Two of these were busy in the Atlantic, two in the Indian Ocean, and a fifth in the Pacific. Disguised as they were—from a distance they looked like harmless merchantmen—they did a great deal of damage. Among them, they sank or captured thirty-six ships in less than three months.

There were also surface warships like the pocket battleships *Graf Spee, Scheer,* and *Deutschland.* Admiral Raeder constantly tried to build and use a strong surface navy, and early in the war he sent out the *Graf Spee* and *Deutschland* to harass the Atlantic lifeline. The *Deutschland* was very cautious and kept away from convoys and trouble. In two and a half months, she sank only two ships and then sneaked home. The *Graf Spee,* however, kept popping in and out of sight, sinking one or two ships each time. She was finally outguessed and trapped by a British force of four cruisers off the coast of South America, in December, 1939. After a deadly fight that lasted an hour and twenty minutes, during which the *Graf Spee*'s big guns did terrible damage to the smaller cruisers, the German ship got to the neutral port of Montevideo, in Uruguay. More British warships were being sent to catch her; she could neither stay in port nor escape, so her commander blew her up and sank her.

The *Scheer* was somewhat luckier than her sister ships. At the end of October, 1940, she sailed out to attack the North Atlantic convoys. Early in November she came upon a single ship, a straggler from a convoy, which she caught and sank. An hour later she sighted the rest—a group of thirty-seven ships with only one escort, the armed merchant cruiser H.M.S. *Jervis Bay*. Captain Fegen, commanding the *Jervis Bay,* realized that he must hold the battleship for as long as he could, so that the convoy could get away. After sending a radio message giving his position, he steamed out to meet the much bigger ship. The engagement, which lasted almost three hours, was completely one-sided. The *Scheer* opened fire at 18,000 yards. The *Jervis Bay* could not get close enough to hit the enemy with her old guns. The cruiser finally went down with a loss of more than two hundred officers and men, among them her brave captain. But the convoy, meantime, had scattered in the darkness. The *Scheer* was able to find and sink only five of them. She then set out southward to look for easy prey in the waters of the Caribbean and the South Atlantic. After five months, she returned home having accounted single-handed for sixteen ships, destroyed or captured.

The British Navy was spread thin. England's fleet could not be everywhere at once, and the submarines and surface ships of the enemy struck at will, sending down ship after ship. "Beating the U-boat," said Mr. Churchill in a message to President Roosevelt, "is simply a question of destroyers and escorts, but we are so

strained that to fill one gap is to open another."
Yet if Britain was to continue her fight, there
must be no end to the supplies that were sent to
her. "Give us arms," said the English, "and we'll
do the job."

And it was clear to America that if Britain
lost her fight the United States, though still a
neutral, would be in grave danger. In a radio
broadcast to the nation, the President said so-
berly, "If Britain should go down, all of us . . .
would be living at the point of a gun. We must
produce arms and ships with every energy and
resource we can command. . . . We must be
the great arsenal of Democracy."

3

The Convoy System

There was no question of America's willingness to be the arsenal of democracy—to build planes, tanks, and guns, and to furnish the ammunition, oil, and gasoline for them. American business and industry buckled down to the task at once. But the goods had to get to the front lines. This was for a long time England's sole responsibility. It meant larger convoys with better protection.

A naval convoy is simply a group of ships traveling together for protection. Its principle is the same as that of the covered-wagon trains going west: one settler in a wagon might travel faster than another, but if hostile Indians attacked him he would be hard put to it to defend himself. One merchant ship might sail faster than another, but her speed would mean little if a submarine attacked. Naturally each single merchant ship could not be defended by a warship. But a group of ships—twenty or thirty—could be defended by a small unit of swift, powerful warships. Even though they could only travel at the speed of the slowest vessel in the group, all together they would have a better chance of coming through in safety.

The convoy system was nothing new in history. In the Middle Ages, merchant ships almost always traveled in company so that their combined armaments would give them better protection against pirates or hostile vessels. The same practice was followed in later years by Spanish treasure fleets coming from the New

World, by Hanseatic and Venetian merchant-men, and by the ships of several countries in the war against Napoleon. It was not until the First World War, however, that the convoy system was brought to a peak of real efficiency.

Germany, in 1917, declared a state of unre-stricted submarine warfare. This meant that submarines would fire on any merchant vessel at sight, and usually without warning. During the first two months of this campaign an average of more than twenty ships a week were destroyed. Everything was tried—camouflage, arming of merchantmen, special routes—everything but the convoy system. Although it seemed a sensible precaution, there was a great deal of opposition to the convoy, mostly from shipowners and the skippers of merchant ships.

They claimed that there would be too many delays in waiting for enough ships to gather be-fore starting out. They argued that a large group of ships would make a larger target for torpedoes and if there were slow ships in the convoy they would all have to travel so slowly that they could never escape attack. Others said that it would be impossible for ships of different speeds and sizes to keep the proper distance and prevent collision, and that in any case there weren't enough warships to give them all protection.

In spite of all the objections, it seemed in the end that the convoy system was the only hope of getting supplies across to the front in Europe, and of bringing troops and weapons across the sea from America. And so, at last, two convoys were tried as an experiment. Both came through without a single ship lost.

This was proof enough. From that moment on, the convoy system was established. And only a tiny fraction of all the ships that traveled in convoy in World War I were sunk.

This same system was consequently put into effect as soon as World War II began. Oddly enough, even though the convoy had already proved its value, there were still skippers who didn't like it. For protection, to make themselves harder to find, convoys changed their course frequently, or zigzagged. Some captains said that there was more danger from crashing into other ships when changing course, than from meeting submarines. But these lone wolves usually suffered: they could not protect themselves against attack, and they couldn't go fast enough to escape. It was not long before even to them it was clear that there was safety in numbers.

Generally convoys consisted of a core of merchant ships, as few as fifteen or as many as sixty, escorted by a team of warships. The warships were usually the smaller types, from destroyers down to cutters and corvettes, since big ships such as cruisers could not maneuver swiftly enough against submarines. The *screen* was that part of the escort equipped with special echo-ranging apparatus—called *sonar* by the Americans and *asdic* by the British—for searching out submarines under the water. In addition to their surface guns, these ships were armed with depth charges for sinking the submarines once they were located. Other vessels of the escort might be armed specially for protection against aircraft, or against enemy ships of war. Later, small aircraft carriers were included in the escort.

There were two officers in command: the Escort Commander, whose job was the safety of the whole group, and who was therefore in overall command; and the Convoy Commodore, who sailed in a merchant ship and was responsible for the discipline of the convoy proper.

The routes of different convoys were known by code letters. For instance, "HX" meant they sailed from Halifax, Nova Scotia, to the United Kingdom, and "SC" meant they sailed from Sydney, Nova Scotia, to England. From the beginning, the HX convoys were the faster ones, while the slower ships were sent in the SC convoys. It was an HX convoy—HX-94—which was guarded by the *Jervis Bay* and broken up by the *Scheer*.

Once the route of a convoy had been decided on, a conference would be held by the Convoy Commander and the Escort Commander for the masters of the merchant ships sailing with them. There, instructions on the route would be

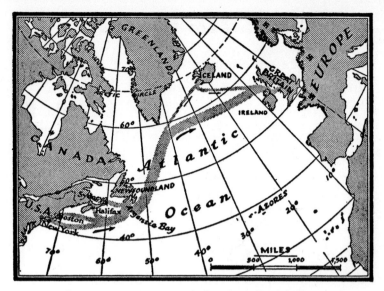

Convoy routes to Iceland and England

handed out; the Comconvoy and Comescort in their blue or khaki navy uniforms would face the tough skippers, most of whom wore only civilian clothes, and give them last-minute instructions. They would be warned about keeping radio silence, holding station, and keeping their ships dark at night. There would be questions and some discussion. Then the Commodore would say, "Good sailing! And good luck!"

A few hours later, the ships would steam out. They might be in nine or ten columns, covering

31

an area of ocean more than four miles wide and a mile and a half long. By day the cutters or corvettes of the screen patrolled in regular patterns on the fringes of the convoy. The little ships pitched and bucked in the rough North Atlantic. Now and then a merchantman would straggle far behind, or another, too eager, would romp ahead. Then the signal light would blink from the Comconvoy's bridge: "Number twelve. Take station!"

At night would come the worst of the journey. Then the darkened ships would be invisible against the pitchy water. No lights were permitted, for even the tiny glow of a cigarette might be enough to reveal their position to lurking submarines. The screen would close in, each ship keeping position on some nearby merchantman. The escort commander would snatch a restless hour of sleep, ready at any moment for the watch officer to call him, always prepared for the sudden crash of an explosion that might tell of a torpedoed ship. The steady pinging of the echo-ranging apparatus would go on and on, searching the depths for any sign of the enemy. Then, if there was no attack, morning would show the ships still in station, bows rising and dipping, throwing up white spray, keeping their orderly pattern on the gray sea.

The early convoys were escorted by Canadian ships to a mid-ocean meeting point, called MOMP, where the British escorts took over. They also had protection by air for several hundred miles out of Halifax, if the weather permitted, and this was taken up again in the Western approaches to England by the Royal Air Force. But the planes could cover only a small part of the route, and there were not enough escort vessels to do a thorough job. There was a wide waste of empty water between England and North America, and in it the submarines prowled and struck. One convoy after another was hit. HX-65 lost seven ships, then HX-72 lost eleven ships and two damaged. HX-90 was attacked five times in twenty-four hours with eleven ships sunk, one of them an escort. There were many dangers for the convoys to face: fog, air attack, magnetic mines that were drawn to a ship's propellers, disguised German raiders, and surface vessels like the *Scheer*. But all of these faded away before the threat sailors feared most: the submarine. More and more, the Atlantic battle focused on an enemy that was powerful, deadly, and invisible.

4

The Undersea Boats

Of all the deceptive appearances in the war, one of the most deceiving was that of the submarines. Most of them were small—only two-thirds the length of a Destroyer Escort, and carrying only a quarter as many men. On deck they might have a four-barreled anti-aircraft gun, a couple of smaller cannon, and a pair of machine guns. On the surface of the water they could barely be seen: their decks were almost level with the waves and only the conning tower stuck up a little way. One of them approaching a group of thirty large cargo ships guarded by sleek destroyers might make you think of a man on a bicycle attacking a herd of elephants. Your thought would be wrong.

The submarine, of whatever country, was developed for sneak attacks. Its crew had to be courageous and determined, but the work they did was treacherous. Their job was to creep close to an unsuspecting ship and without warning or quarter blow it up with a special underwater shell called a torpedo. German submarines, called U-boats (for the German word *Unterseeboot,* or undersea boat), were fast and skillful. They were dark gray, like shadows in the sea. In arctic waters they might be painted white to look like icebergs. They were hard to spot, harder to catch. Slipping inside the guard of a convoy, they could release four torpedoes from the bow in less than that many minutes, and be gone while the shattered pieces of ships were still falling into the water.

The submarine was not a German invention, although some people think so because in both World Wars Germany used it so intensively. The first underwater boat was made by a Hollander, Cornelius van Drebel, in 1620. Submarines were not used against warships with any success until the Civil War when a blockade ship, *Housatonic,* was sunk by a wooden craft floating under the surface with an explosive charge fastened to its bows. Actually, Germany was one of the last countries to take the submarine seriously; it was not until 1906, almost ten years after America and France had adopted them, that the Germans accepted U-boats as part of the navy.

The submarine is a cigar-shaped vessel with two hulls. The inner hull is strong and thick, made to withstand the pressure of tons of sea water. Outside this is another hull, and the space between consists of tanks of fuel oil and of compressed air. The air tanks keep the ship floating, but when they are slowly filled with sea water they add weight and allow the ship to sink under the surface. Hydroplanes, or flaps that can be tilted fore and aft, send the ship up or down, just as the flaps of an airplane do. When the tanks are "blown"—that is, when water is forced out of them by compressed air—the ship becomes light and buoyant once more.

The most widely used U-boat was Type VIIC, of 700 tons displacement. (The tonnage of a warship is stated in terms of the vessel's weight, and is generally called displacement.) Type VIIC was 220 feet long and twenty feet wide. It had four bow torpedo tubes and one stern tube, and carried fourteen torpedoes.

The speed of a ship is stated in knots and a vessel traveling one knot covers one nautical mile—6,080 feet—in one hour. The U-boat Type VIIC could travel at about eight knots under water, but on the surface it could make eighteen knots (or eighteen nautical miles an hour). This was fast enough to catch any convoy. It could

dive to almost four hundred feet, and some submarine commanders claimed to have gone to
twice that depth. Although its deck guns were
small compared to those of a Destroyer Escort,
for example, they were large enough to sink
most merchant vessels. As the war went on,
larger and more powerful subs were put into
action, although fortunately the largest and
fastest of all were not produced in time to help
the Germans. Also, late in the war new inventions were introduced. One of these was the
Schnorchel (shortened by us to *snorkel*), which
was a special breathing tube that allowed
U-boats to stay under water as long as they
wished until their fuel gave out.

Inside, the submarine was a crowded and
cramped maze of machinery and equipment. In
the center was the control room, containing the
periscope machinery underneath the conning
tower, as well as all the apparatus that was used
when the boat was submerged. Near by were
radar and radio offices, the switchboard, and the
chart room. Among all the tangle of pipes, valves,

dials, and engines, lived some forty-five men. Their bunks were collapsible, and at mealtimes the upper ones were raised so that the men could sit on the lower ones along the table. To save space, there were fewer bunks than there were crew members. As soon as a man went on watch another man would be able to go to sleep in his bed. A VIIC boat could cruise for 8,500 miles without refueling, and during the three months of a cruise men lived under the most difficult conditions. There was no room for anything but the simplest necessities, and when a man wasn't doing his regular job, or sleeping, he took his turn at cleaning the ship or doing K.P. Sometimes, if the weather was warm and the sun bright, some of the crew might sun-bathe on deck. But many submarines paid the price for such relaxation by being attacked by planes and bombed while the conning tower hatches were open and the crew in swimming.

The basic weapon of the submarine was, of course, the torpedo, which is a kind of miniature submarine in itself. It, too, is cigar-shaped, with a warhead containing about 500 pounds of TNT. Although this torpedo was only some twenty-four feet long it could, if it hit a vital spot, destroy a tanker five hundred feet long that weighed hundreds of tons. The torpedo had an air chamber for keeping it buoyant, a gyroscope for balance, a little motor to drive it, its own fuel, and steering vanes in its tail. It could be set to run at different depths, and could be adjusted to take its own course, quite different from that of the submarine itself. The motor left a train of bubbles behind it by which the torpedo might be spotted and sometimes dodged. However, it wasn't long before electrically driven torpedoes began to be used, and they could not be seen in this way.

The U-boat's tactics, at first, were to cruise on the surface, usually alone, keeping in touch with its base by radio and waiting for word of a convoy. It made a tiny target on the surface, and if a scouting plane should spot it, it could quickly dive deep. It could stay under water for two days, if necessary, only having to come to the surface after that time to change its air and charge the batteries. This operation might take two or three hours.

When word came of a fat flock of "sheep," the U-boat would slip in softly, on the surface if it was dark. It trailed the convoy, waiting for a chance to get close enough.

To see a convoy from inside a submarine is to see it with the tense eye of the hunter. The merchantmen can barely be seen as dark looming shapes against the sky. The range and bearing of a cargo ship is plotted automatically. When set, the torpedo officer shouts, "Tubes one to five, ready!"

The U-boat commander, waiting for the right moment, watching patiently, gives his command to the torpedo officer: "Fire at 1,000 meters."

The torpedo officer peers through the attack sight and gets the target in the cross hairs. She may be a tanker, loaded with tons of oil, or a cargo ship carrying tanks and ammunition and wallowing heavily in the sea.

"Hard to starboard," says the commander. "Fire when ready."

"Ready——" The torpedo officer holds the image of the ship in his sights. "Fire!" He presses the firing button.

The whole boat shudders . . . and again . . . and again, and the hiss of compressed air is heard as the torpedoes speed away. The seconds pass. On the merchant ship the men are unconscious of the danger. The watch on the bridge is scanning the dark sea, and the men off duty down below are playing cards, sleeping, or writing letters.

Then suddenly there is a roar. A brilliant orange flame rises, a billowing cloud of smoke, there are smaller flashes, and the thud of explosion. The nearest escort, with her sirens whooping and her crew at battle stations, screams to the spot. Depth charges fly overboard, sending up fountains of water. The submarine has already dived, going far down, silent and slow, trying to escape the bombs.

This was the hardest part of the maneuver for the U-boat. For when the escorts counterattacked, a kind of deadly game of blindman's buff would begin, a battle in which neither side could see the enemy. They could hear each other by means of a special listening device called "sonar," and when the captain of an escort vessel thought he was right over the submarine he would drop depth charges. He had to try to set these charges to explode at the correct depth, which meant more guesswork. The U-boat captain, in his turn, when he thought his enemy was right over him, would change his course and try to slide away. He would move to different depths, too, and unless a depth charge exploded right next to him, he might be shaken but not seriously damaged. On the other hand, if the hulls of a submarine were pierced, it was much harder to find and stop a leak than it was in a surface ship.

Sometimes, to escape, the U-boat would release a *pillenwerfer*. This was a mass of small gas bubbles which gave an echo on the sonar machine similar to that of the submarine. While the escort was dropping depth charges on the "pill" the submarine would quietly slip away.

During the first months of the war, matters hung in the balance. There were not many vessels for escort duty, nor were there enough long-range airplanes to give adequate air cover to the convoys. To compensate for this, however, it was hard for the U-boats out in the wide ocean to find their prey, and once they had found it the increasingly skillful use of sonar by escort ships kept the U-boat down where it could not attack properly. So, at last, a new tactic was developed by the chief of the German submarine command, Rear Admiral Karl Doenitz. This was the "wolf pack" tactic.

Doenitz was to become the worst enemy the Allies had upon the seas. Although at the beginning he was only in command of submarines and was four ranks below Admiral Raeder, the naval commander in chief, he won Hitler's attention and admiration. He was a ruthless, daring, and capable officer, who did not hesitate to tell his captains to shoot helpless sailors in the water so they could not ship out again. Eventually he took Raeder's place as chief of the fleet, and it was his brilliance and efficiency that made the Atlantic battle such a long, hard one.

From his base at Lorient, in France, he kept contact with all the U-boats at sea. These boats were sent out in a great fan in groups of ten or twenty. The sub that first made contact with a convoy would act as "shadower," reporting back by radio. In this way, "Papa" Doenitz, who knew where every U-boat was, could send in all the members of the pack who were in the area. The shadower would keep some distance from the convoy, waiting for the rest of the pack to arrive and estimating where the convoy would be by nightfall. Then, in the dark, the wolves would meet; silently they would surface, fire their torpedoes and then dive. The escorts could not be everywhere at once, nor could they follow every trail. Half an hour later, when things were quiet, the pack would attack again. So it would go, not once or twice, but hour after hour, all through the night and even through the next day.

There was only one answer to this tactic. More and better escort vessels were needed, with trained crews working together as a unit to make the best use of their weapons, to destroy submarines and bring the convoys through. Unfortunately, hundreds of good ships and men were to be drowned and lost before this goal was reached.

5

The Short-of-war War

The first two years of the war, from the fall of France in 1939, until the bombing of Pearl Harbor in 1941, were not altogether one-sided. The U-boats never ceased their operations, and their numbers steadily increased, but at the same time England developed and expanded her bases in Canada and Iceland, and routed convoys so as to get maximum protection. Both England

and Canada increased their escort fleets. Corvettes, sloops, and frigates were built: these were seaworthy little ships, equipped to catch and sink submarines. They were hard-working and uncomfortable. When a man said, "I'm in corvettes," other sailors kept a respectful silence.

Escort groups were trained that worked under more or less permanent commanders. These groups had a strong team spirit, and developed their own methods of work. Early in March, 1941, submarine U-47 was killed by one of these groups, and when she went down she carried with her her commander, Gunther Prien, one of the U-boat aces. Nine days later U-99 and U-100 were destroyed; their captains were also aces. Few of the U-boat captains were the equals of these three for ability and daring, and their loss was a great blow to Germany.

But England's strength was still small for the size of the job that had to be done. In March, April, and May of 1941 the U-boats alone sank 142 ships of 818,000 tons. To put this figure in more understandable words: when a sub sank two big cargo ships and one medium oil tanker, a total of 15,000 tons, the loss was equal to 42 tanks, 8 six-inch howitzers, 88 twenty-five-pound guns, 40 two-pound guns, 24 armored cars, 50 Bren gun carriers, 5,210 tons of ammunition, 600 rifles, 428 tons of tank supplies, 2,000 tons of stores, and 1,000 tanks of gasoline. To knock out the same amount of equipment by an air bombing, the enemy would have had to make *three thousand* successful flights. It is easy to see that every convoy attacked meant terrible losses that lengthened the war.

The United States was helping to replace these losses. Fifty destroyers had been swapped to Britain for naval bases; arms and ammunition were sent on Lend-Lease; a great ship-building program had been started, and American waters were being patrolled. America was giving Britain all the help possible short of actually going to war.

To ensure that supplies would get at least halfway over the ocean, the United States government, in April of 1941, drew a line between the Eastern and Western Hemispheres and declared that this marked the American sea frontier. It ran along the meridian of 26° west, dividing the Atlantic in half. Within the western half, it was announced, we would defend our own ships, and our patrols were extended up to that line.

Hitler had no wish to violate American neutrality, for he knew that if the United States was drawn into the war he would be facing great odds. Many of the German naval officers were in favor of sending U-boats close to the coast of the United States, and of shooting at American vessels, but Hitler forbade it. In fact, submarine commanders complained that their leader's caution made things difficult for them; they were sometimes afraid to fire at destroyers which might turn out to be flying the American flag. Sometimes, however, "mistakes" were made.

In May, 1941, President Roosevelt declared an Unlimited National Emergency. "The war," he said, "is approaching the brink of the Western Hemisphere. It is coming very close to home."

Only three days later, to prove him right, U-boats sank nine ships carrying lend-lease goods to Britain. They did this just off Cape Farewell, Greenland, well inside the line of the American sea frontier.

The next step was to extend the frontier to include that stepping stone—Iceland—which Britain had so far held. In July the First Brigade (reinforced) of Marines was formed, suddenly issued woolen underwear, and sent to take over the defense of Iceland from the British. Soon after, Task Force 1 was organized to escort convoys of the United States and Iceland. One sentence of its orders read, ". . . including shipping of any nationality which may join such United States or Iceland flag convoys." This gave the ships of other nations a chance to join the neutral convoys, for protection. Our navy then began escort duty with these convoys, while England continued to take charge of the transatlantic route.

Soon after, a United States destroyer, *Greer*, was fired on by a submarine while approaching

Iceland. She dodged two torpedoes and counter-attacked with depth charges, but the U-boat escaped. It was the first shot in an undeclared war. President Roosevelt then issued what was called the "shoot first" order, in which he said, "From now on, if German or Italian vessels of war enter the waters the protection of which is necessary for American defense they do so at their own peril. The orders I have given as Commander in Chief to the United States Army and Navy are to carry out that policy at once."

American neutrality and patience were wearing out. Congress passed two amendments to the Neutrality Act, one which allowed merchant ships to arm themselves, and one which permitted them to enter zones of war. In September, 1941, direct protection was given to the Halifax convoys by American escorts for the first time. There were now five times as many U-boats in the Atlantic as there had been in 1940.

The major burden still lay on England, however. For every American who saw that sooner or later we would be drawn into the fight, there were others who thought we could hold aloof. They still saw the United States as an island, separated from the rest of the world by two oceans. Within three months, that illusion was to be ended at Pearl Harbor.

6

A-hunting We Will Go

The English escort commanders learned the hard way, developing the tactics of antisubmarine warfare, perfecting teams, and bringing the convoys through in spite of everything the Germans could throw at them. The courage and craft of these British officers can nowhere be seen clearer than in the work of Commander Walker, Royal Navy.

Frederic J. Walker was a tall, lean man of forty-five when he took command of H.M.S. *Stork* as captain and senior officer of the 36th Escort Group. This square-jawed man, whose deep-set eyes could twinkle with merriment as he told jokes over a glass of beer in the wardroom, or turn cold as ice as he stood on the bridge watching for the enemy, was one of the Royal Navy's first specialists in antisubmarine warfare. He had been at sea since the age of seventeen, seen action during the First World War, and had taken part in the evacuation from Dunkirk. Almost from the moment he came aboard the *Stork* he showed his determination to make his escort group into a tight-knit team, the best in the service.

Under his command were two sloops, *Stork* and *Deptford,* and seven smaller corvettes of the "Flower" class—that is, they were named after flowers: *Gardenia, Marigold,* and so on. In spite of their sweet names, they were grim fighters.

On the very first convoy, which was to Gibraltar, Walker began by developing plans for combined operations in which all the ships of his team would deal systematically with any submarine that might attack. There were plans for searching an area, for guarding the convoy, and for counterattack. He started depth-charge-loading competitions between ships, and gunnery practice competitions. At night, when the crews were worn out, Walker would dash up alongside one of the ships of his group in a motorboat and yell, "Officer of the Day! You've just been torpedoed aft, a fire has broken out, and the enemy is crossing your bows! What do you do now?" This sort of relentless testing was hard to put up with, but it paid off later, a thousand times, in action.

One of Walker's first plans for fighting U-boats was called "Operation Buttercup." It was based on his experience that submarines generally attacked a convoy at night, on the surface, and remained near the wreck of a torpedoed ship or else went off at high speed, still on the surface. "Operation Buttercup"—named after his wife's nickname—called for the use of searchlights, rockets, and star shells to light up the darkness and thus force the U-boat to submerge. Under the surface it would have to move more slowly, and then the escort ships would plaster the whole area with depth charges. This gave them a better chance of sinking the sub. The plan was later adopted by the Admiralty.

Walker's hard work in making his group into a fighting unit paid off with Convoy HG-76. Attacked by eight or nine U-boats on the way to Gibraltar, the convoy pushed on through a running battle that lasted for several days and nights, and Walker's 36th Group sank U-131, U-434, and U-574. In the case of U-574, the submarine was forced to come to the surface because depth-charge explosions had badly damaged her. She popped up not more than 200 yards from the *Stork,* Walker's own ship, and at once turned to port and began circling.

As usual in one of Walker's operations, the night was bright with snowflake rockets and searchlights. In this ghastly illumination, the sub circled, keeping inside the *Stork*'s larger turning circle. The sloop was so close to the U-boat that she could not use her four-inch guns, for they couldn't be pointed downward sharply enough to hit the small, close target. All the *Stork*'s men could do was curse helplessly and fire off small arms. The first lieutenant hung over the bow rails with a submachine gun and riddled the U-boat's conning tower.

Then, at the third circle, Walker put the *Stork*'s helm hard over. With a grinding crash, he rammed the submarine just in front of the conning tower. The U-boat slid all the way down the keel of the sloop, and when she tore free at the stern, the *Stork* blasted her with depth charges. U-574's captain went down with his ship.

For this, and other successful actions, Walker was eventually made commander of a unique outfit, the 2nd Support Group. The Germans had thrown a long line of U-boats right across the convoy route in the North Atlantic. The 2nd

Support Group's job was not primarily to bring convoys through, but to go out and sink submarines and break through their line.

The group made several successful hunts, including one record breaker that lasted for fifteen hours. Then they were sent to waylay U-boats that were leaving the Bay of Biscay and, after a successful season there, were sent north again in 1943. It was in the North Atlantic that one of Walker's most exciting chases took place.

His team now consisted of five sloops, all of a class named for birds: *Starling* (Walker's flagship), *Kite, Wild Goose, Magpie,* and *Woodcock*. These were the best and biggest antisubmarine vessels available at the time. Also in the group was a small airplane carrier, *Tracker*. Their mission was to cover convoys between Iceland and the Azores, and also to find and smash U-boats wherever they could.

On the first day of November the weather, which was already rough, turned stormy. High winds and waves tore gun mountings from the decks and smashed lifeboats to bits. Then slowly the storm cleared. At night, the *Kite,* which had joined the team late, reported to Walker by radio-telephone that there was a U-boat on the surface two miles ahead. Walker instructed the *Kite* to trail the submarine until morning. The carrier *Tracker* was to keep clear of the danger area with *Magpie* and *Wild Goose* as her screen; the *Woodcock* was to join the *Starling* and *Kite* in the attack.

In the morning, however, contact was lost. Walker, in a patched old jacket, and the dirty turtle-neck sweater he always wore, stood on the *Starling*'s bridge with a sandwich in one hand and his binoculars in the other. He realized that the U-boat had released a "pill" and that the *Kite*'s asdic, or echo-ranging gear, had been diverted by it. Searching carefully, he picked up the sub again on his own asdic and at seven in the morning gave instructions to the other two ships with him by loudspeaker, so that the U-boat could not pick up his message. The *Starling* would keep the sub's position fixed. The *Woodcock* would go in for the first attack, the

Kite for the second. When they were very close to the U-boat, the noise of their own motors would blanket the sub's location on the asdic, so the *Starling* would coach them in and give the necessary commands by radio-telephone.

Lieutenant Commander Gwinner, in the *Woodcock,* said to his men, "I expect to sink the enemy before breakfast." Then, with his asdic silent and his motors just turning over, he glided in over the spot where the U-boat lay submerged. Just before the ranges and bearings of the sloop and the submarine coincided, Walker yelled into the radio-telephone, "Fire *now!*"

Twenty-six depth charges were shot over the side. Walker, watching, said, "I'll stake my last penny on a decisive result to that attack." He won. U-220 never came to the surface again.

Two hours later, the group fastened on another sub. Both the *Magpie* and the *Wild Goose* were complaining that they had been left out of the fun, so Walker gave them the nod: "Go in there and blow his breeches off!" But this time there was nothing but trouble. The first depth-charge run was too far away from the U-boat. Upon checking his gyrocompass, Walker found that it had been thrown off by the explosions. The *Wild Goose* went in for a second attack, and this time when Walker shouted the command, "Fire now!" the depth charges went over the rail just too late.

Walker threw his cap on the deck and jumped on it. "That was a thoroughly bum attack!" he roared. "I'll bet my last penny it failed miserably." He was just about to send a sharp message to Lieutenant Commander Wemyss, the unhappy captain of the *Wild Goose,* when suddenly they heard the unmistakable *crunch* of a submarine breaking up underwater. Then oil, a headless torpedo, and various bits of debris spread over the sea. It was the end of U-842.

When the group returned to the base at Argentia, Newfoundland, after weathering another terrible storm, the band on the dock played, "A-hunting we will go." By now, this had become Walker's theme song.

The long hours on the bridge in all sorts of

weather, the overstrain, the lack of sleep and proper meals, the great weariness of fighting year after year, did what the enemy had never been able to do. Commander Walker died on Sunday, July 9, 1944, of a heart attack.

Winston Churchill said, "In my opinion, no single officer at sea did more than Frederic Walker to win this battle [against the U-boat], the hardest and longest drawn out of the war." Admiral Sir Max Horton, Commander in Chief of the Western Approaches, said, "Victory has been won and should be won by such as he."

But for the men who followed Walker, and under his command totaled the high score of twenty-two submarines destroyed, the best words would be those of Samuel Eliot Morison, biographer of our own navy in the Second World War. He wrote, "The hunting was apt to be poor for anyone else when Walker was about."

7

The Chase of the Bismarck

It was well for England—and for those who were to be her allies—that she had many men like Commander Walker. But not all the fighting was against the undersea enemy. In May, 1941, one of the few engagements between big surface vessels in the Atlantic took place, and was to prove very important to the course of the war.

In spite of treaty limitations before the war,

Germany had been secretly building warships of greater size than any other country's. Among these were the battle cruisers *Scharnhorst* and *Gneisenau,* and the three pocket battleships *Scheer, Deutschland,* and the ill-fated *Graf Spee,* which had been scuttled by her own captain early in the war. Furthermore, there were the two battleships *Bismarck* and *Tirpitz,* which were the biggest ships in the world at the time they were launched. With their heavy armor and big guns, they were a powerful threat to convoys, for they could blast the smaller escort vessels out of the water at long range and smash cargo ships to matchwood.

Late in May, word came to the British command that the giant *Bismarck,* in company with another ship, the battlecruiser *Prinz Eugen,* had been spotted moving in the Baltic Sea. There were eleven convoys, including a troop convoy, either at sea or just about to sail. It was clear that the Germans were planning a raid.

At once, the British Home Fleet under Admiral Sir John Tovey was sent out to search for the enemy. Prime Minister Churchill sent the news to President Roosevelt and asked that the United States Navy, although neutral, help by marking the position of the German ships if they should slip through the hands of the British. Anxious hours followed, and then at last the Germans were spotted at the very edge of the ice pack, northwest of Iceland. They were heading south toward the convoy lanes.

Admiral Tovey, in his flagship *King George V*, made all speed with his main force to catch them. Two of his ships, *Hood* and *Prince of Wales*, steamed up from the south and were the first to meet the enemy. Within a few minutes the *Hood*, England's largest and swiftest capital ship, had been hit and blown up, while the *Prince of Wales*, a new ship, had been damaged and forced to fall back.

The *Bismarck*, however, had not come out of the engagement untouched. She had been hit below the waterline and one of her oil tanks had been pierced. The oil left a plain trail behind her on the sea, which could be spotted from the air. But she was still more than a match for any other ship afloat. If she escaped, it would be a major victory for Germany.

Admiral Tovey, with the rest of his ships, among them the carrier *Victorious,* still tried to close with her. The cruisers *Norfolk* and *Suffolk,* with the *Prince of Wales* still grimly hanging on, used their radar to shadow the *Bismarck.* And from the south other British ships were summoned: *Rodney* and *Ramillies* drawn away from convoy duty, and from Gibraltar the battle cruiser *Renown* and the aircraft carrier *Ark Royal.* Slowly, the British net was being drawn about the fleeing German battleship.

On the evening of the twenty-fourth, the *Bismarck* suddenly turned and fought back at her pursuers. Under cover of this action, her companion, the smaller *Prinz Eugen,* made off at high speed and eventually got safely to a French port. The night was dark with squalls of wind and rain, but even so airplanes from the carrier *Victorious* flew out and torpedoed the

Bismarck. The German ship was hit once, but not seriously damaged. Then, in the early hours of the morning, contact with her was lost.

The next twenty-four hours were black ones. Admiral Tovey believed that the *Bismarck* was heading for the North Sea, but by evening it was clear she must be making for the port of Brest, in the south. It was also clear that she had slipped through the net and was far to the east of the British flagship. The only hope lay in the ships from Gibraltar which were plowing up through heavy seas to intercept her.

In England the air was tense. The House of Commons was to meet on the twenty-seventh of May, and it would be a sad blow to morale if they had to be told that the German battleship, after sinking the *Hood* and wounding the *Prince of Wales,* had got away safely to attack convoys another time. The Admiralty had planes out searching the Atlantic, but meanwhile fuel in the British ships was running low and several of them had had to reduce speed.

Admiral Tovey's flagship, *King George V,* had only about another ten hours of steaming time left.

Then, at the very last moment, 10:30 A.M. on Monday the twenty-sixth, a plane located the *Bismarck* again. She was seven hundred miles from Brest, still going strong but not yet within the German air cover that was based on the French shore.

The carrier *Ark Royal* closed in to within forty miles and sent fifteen Swordfish torpedo planes aloft. But war is full of confusion by its very nature. The planes' radar led them to the British cruiser *Sheffield* and they attacked her by mistake. Fortunately the *Sheffield* was able to dodge, and the airplanes, signaling "Sorry for the kipper!" returned to the carrier to rearm. The next time there was no mistake. They found the *Bismarck* and torpedoed her. With her rudder jammed, the big ship was out of control. Shortly before midnight, her commander reported to his base: "Ship unmaneuverable. We shall fight to the last shell."

Admiral Tovey had only a couple of hours left before his fuel gave out. But headquarters radioed him to go on with the chase even if he had to be towed home. The *Bismarck* by now was moving directly away from the coast. Surrounding her were one Polish and four British destroyers, the battleships *King George V* and *Rodney*, and the cruisers *Dorsetshire* and *Norfolk*. And from the other side, U-boats and heavy bombers were on the way to help the *Bismarck*.

In the teeth of a northwesterly gale, the British closed in. At 8:47 A.M. on the 27th the *Rodney* opened fire, followed by the *King George V*. The *Bismarck*'s heavy guns were still working, and although her crew were dropping with weariness they returned the fire. But the British attack was too strong. After an hour and a half, the *Bismarck*'s weapons were silent, and the ship herself was a battered, flaming wreck. The cruiser *Dorsetshire* ran in close and torpedoed her. Slowly she turned over, her flag still flying, and then reared high and dived to the bottom. Almost all the crew, including the German admiral, disappeared along with the battleship.

The effects of this battle were felt at once. The *Bismarck*'s sister ship, the giant *Tirpitz,* was now alone and the Germans were very cautious about using her. With both battleships in action, they might have seriously injured the northern convoys. The threat was still there, but it was cut in half.

Equally important was the sharp lesson learned: that modern sea warfare was no longer a case of two ships fighting it out. The new and valuable weapon, radar, had been used to trail the *Bismarck*. Teamwork by different vessels had trapped her. And it was a combination of sea and air attack that had finished her. The part played by radar and by aircraft carriers was to be vital in winning the battle of the Atlantic.

8

Fateful Events

For America, at least, the sinking of the *Bismarck* brought home another kind of lesson, one that made for thoughtful faces in the Department of the Navy. For the United States did not have one single vessel capable of meeting the *Bismarck* or the *Tirpitz* on anything like equal terms. And the *Tirpitz,* now going through her trial runs and last-minute adjustments, was soon to be ready for sea duty.

The situation was made even sharper by two other events in the same month of May. A neutral passenger ship, S.S. *ZamZam,* was sunk by a German raider. Aboard her were about 150 United States citizens on their way home. Then, three days before the *Bismarck* battle, an American merchant ship, S.S. *Robin Moor,* was torpedoed "by accident" in the South Atlantic by a U-boat. The war was coming closer and closer to America.

The great Nazi war machine, with its partner Italy, had now rolled over all of Europe. Norway, Denmark, Holland, Belgium, and France had fallen; Greece, which had resisted bravely, had been conquered; the Balkan countries were either Hitler's allies or his subjects; Spain was outwardly neutral, but secretly furnishing house-room for Nazi spies.

The Soviet Union, whose borders spread from eastern Europe to the Pacific, and from the Arctic circle far to the south, had a treaty with Germany. Nevertheless, Hitler began massing troops all along the Soviet-German border. On the morning of the twenty-second of June, 1941, they struck without warning. Planes bombed ten villages at once, armored columns roared over the Russian opposition in the familiar "blitz" or lightning war. One hundred and sixty-four divisions were thrown into Russia. In one month, the Germans had advanced three hundred miles.

The Soviet government had watched other countries being overrun, but had hoped to keep altogether free of entanglement in the war. The Russians themselves had been guilty of marching into other countries, for the sake, they said, of protecting their own borders. Now they were taken completely by surprise. Most military authorities in England and America believed that the Russian armies would be destroyed in a few months, like those of the other countries Hitler had blitzed. But Russia was an enormous country, and her people were tough fighters. Hitler had expected another Holland or France; instead, the Nazi war machine almost ground to a stop. Behind the German lines organized guerrilla bands rose up. The people burned their crops and houses so that nothing would fall into enemy hands, and then fought to the death. The Russian winter was approaching, and though the Nazis drove on and took one city after another, they still had not reached their major goals.

It now became very important to the United States and Great Britain to see to it that Russia was supplied, so that she could go on holding the German armies. So one more road had to be opened: a sea road north toward the fringe of the pack ice and down to the Russian ports in the Arctic. There were other routes by which supplies were sent to Russia—across the Pacific, for instance, or through the Persian Gulf—but these meant long overland hauls and much more time. The shortest way was over the North Atlantic to Iceland, then through the Barents Sea and down to Murmansk or Archangel. Murmansk was free of ice all year round, and

Archangel for about half the year. A vast net-
work of airfields and a system of weather patrols
operating with icebreakers (ships specially designed to break lanes in the ice with their sharp
metal prows) kept the way clear. It was America's part to send ammunition, oil, machinery,
guns, planes, and vehicles; England, in addition
to sending some of the vital supplies, had the
job of organizing and escorting the convoys.

Hitler had written Mussolini in December,
1940, "The war in the West is in itself won."
But as 1941 drew to a close, it was plain that he
was wrong—and not for the first time. The war
had widened. England, still under heavy air
bombardment every day, was far from crushed.
The British people joked in their air-raid shel-
ters, cleared away the wreckage, and went back
to work. In North Africa a long and savage des-
ert battle ended in the taking of Tobruk, with
a severe setback for the German and Italian
forces. In Russia the bitter winter set in, which
froze airplane and tank motors, automatic weapons, and Germans. The Nazi attack on three

main objectives—Moscow, Leningrad, and the Don Basin in the south—had not been successful. In spite of U-boats and surface ships, supplies still crossed the ocean in one convoy after another.

The war, instead of being over, was only beginning. America was still neutral, but seven American merchant ships had already been sunk. The United States destroyer *Kearny*, guarding an Iceland-bound convoy, had been torpedoed with many casualties. And at dawn on the thirty-first of October, 1941, the first United States Navy ship—U.S.S. *Reuben James* —was lost in a battle of the war that was not yet declared between Germany and America. This is how it happened:

Convoy HX-156 was heading for Iceland. It was still some six hundred miles west of England, escorted by five United States destroyers. In these early days of America's convoy duty, experience was often lacking. The convoy was not zigzagging nor were the destroyers patrolling properly. Suddenly a tremendous explosion was heard. Lieutenant Commander Griffith Coale, a seagoing artist who was on one of the destroyers, later described in his book, *North Atlantic Patrol,* what he saw and heard in those early morning hours:

A mile ahead a rising cloud of dark smoke hangs over the black loom of a ship. With a terrific roar, a column of orange flame towers high into the night as her magazines go up, subsides, leaving a great black pall of smoke licked by moving tongues of orange. All the ship forward of No. 4 stack has disappeared. We move rapidly down upon her, as her stern rises perpendicularly into the air and slides slowly down into the sea. A moment, and two grunting jolts of her depth charges toss debris and men into the air. Suddenly my nostrils are filled with the sickly stench of fuel oil, and the sea is flat and silvery under its thick coating. Before we know it, we hear the cursing, praying, and hoarse shouts for help, and we are all among her men, like black shiny seals in

the oily water . . . "We are the *Reuben James'*
men!" comes a chorus from one raft, and then we
know . . .

To those men in the water, and the sailors
who pulled them out, neutrality was a word that
had lost its meaning. Only 45 of the 160 men
on the *Reuben James* were saved, and one of
those died afterward on the rescue ship.

Thirty-seven days later, American neutrality
ended suddenly and dramatically. Without a
declaration of war, Japan bombed the military
and naval installations at Pearl Harbor.

It was a grave and terrible moment. But it
was a moment of decision, as well. Winston
Churchill wrote of it: "The British Empire, the
Soviet Union, and now the United States, bound
together with every scrap of their life and
strength, were, according to my lights, twice or
even thrice the force of their antagonists. No
doubt it would take a long time. . . . Many dis-
asters . . . lay ahead, but there was no more
doubt about the end."

9

The War Comes to America

The war was now a world war in fact, for every continent had been drawn into it.

At first the attention of the United States was fixed on the Pacific. There, most of the United States Navy had been concentrated, and after the attack on Pearl Harbor the fleet was dispersed and temporarily immobilized. The Japanese invaded the Philippines, and 36,000

American soldiers were killed, wounded, or captured at Bataan alone. Guam, Wake, and Midway islands, stepping stones to the far east, as Greenland and Iceland were to the west, were taken. Japanese forces attacked Burma and Malaya; Hong Kong and Singapore fell to them. It seemed that in the air and on the sea they were victorious.

But at the same time, America had to maintain the flow of supplies to her allies, England and Russia. A year before the United States entered the war there had been a series of secret discussions between the representatives of the British and American chiefs of staff. It had been determined that Germany was the most important of the three Axis powers and that consequently the Atlantic, and the continent of Europe, were to be considered the most decisive theatres of action. During the first months, most of America's fighting was done in the Pacific. But she was still the arsenal of democracy— American factories and farms gave the Allies their greatest advantage over the enemy.

The Nazis believed that the war in the Pacific would draw the United States completely out of the Atlantic. Hitler wanted a quick victory in North Africa, and so most of the available U-boats were sent to the Mediterranean to attack supply and troop convoys going to Africa. Only six U-boats were assigned to make the first assault on the American coast. However, these subs were commanded by expert captains, and America was almost totally unprepared.

All along the Atlantic coast ran the important sea lanes from South American ports, from the oil refineries of the Dutch West Indies, and from the Gulf of Mexico. These lanes touched the river outlets along the seaboard on the route to New York, the greatest port in the world. The defenses were pitiful.

For the first four months of its operations the Eastern Sea Frontier, which stretched from Canada to Florida, had nine short-range army bombers to use for patrolling. To fight the submarines, it had some sixty-five small Coast Guard cutters, a few slow and weak "Eagle" boats from the First World War, some private yachts, and about thirty British armed trawlers. These had to defend a thousand miles of coast. The Gulf Sea Frontier, which included lower Florida, the Gulf of Mexico, and Cuba, had three cutters and a converted yacht. For air cover there were eighteen unarmed Coast Guard planes, fourteen army planes with nothing more than light machine guns, and two medium bombers on the point of falling apart. The Caribbean Sea Frontier, which was the center of shipping for oil and bauxite, a mineral from which aluminum is made, was defended by two destroyers, two old "Eagle" boats, three small submarines, and twelve patrol planes.

Nor was this the only weakness. The vast majority of Americans had no experience of war. Along the coast, many cities failed to dim their lights. In the vacation spots, like Atlantic City or the resorts of Florida, hotel owners complained that a blackout would ruin the tourist trade. The bright signs and street lights furnished a perfect background against which ships were silhouetted at night as easy targets for torpedoes. On the short-wave radio, information of all sorts was released—positions of ships at sea, and the routes and times of patrol planes. There were enemy agents listening to the careless talk of sailors along the waterfronts, and relaying it to submarines at sea. Worst of all, there were no convoys: the traffic consisted of individual ships, unarmed, slow, and helpless.

In his operations room in a villa overlooking the submarine pens at Lorient, Admiral Doenitz had reports of all this and rubbed his hands in satisfaction. Hitler and his other officers were "land minded"—even now they did not fully appreciate the value of sea operations to cut the shipping lanes. Doenitz was about to give them another demonstration. The code word *Drumbeat* was flashed to the waiting U-boats.

The first victim was a British passenger steamer, *Cyclops,* torpedoed and sunk on January 12, 1942, only 300 miles off Cape Cod. A little later on the same day, a Pan-American tanker was sunk in the north, and a Latvian merchant ship further south. Two more tankers followed; then, less than a week later, an American ship, the *Allan Jackson,* carrying a full cargo of crude oil, was torpedoed just off Cape Hatteras, North Carolina. The sea all about the ship blazed as boats and ladders and deck plates crumpled in the heat. Twenty-two men lost their lives in the flaming wreckage.

Altogether, thirteen ships were lost in a little more than two weeks. The first six U-boats were reinforced by the arrival of others, but only fifteen or twenty submarines, on the average, operated along the coast. The Germans became very bold. They often attacked on the surface in broad daylight, and if their torpedoes did not finish off a ship, they would do the job with gunfire. As the torpedoed ship went down, the U-boat sailors, laughing and joking, might snap pictures of the sinking. Sometimes they would scold the crews of merchant ships for being late

A fleet of British destroyers, loaded with troops rescued from the trap at Dunkirk, arrives in England.

Trainees at a German submarine school are shown receiving instruction aboard their ships. This photograph was taken just prior to the Nazi invasion of Poland.

*British Captain Frederic J. Walker shouts encourage-
ment to another sloop in his escort group. (Chapter 6)*

*Corvettes, such as the British K-327 shown here, proved
to be extremely valuable for convoy escort duty.*

Twin geysers shoot skyward as a U.S. Navy PC boat drops two depth charges which explode simultaneously. These speedy little patrol craft fought valiantly to drive the German submarines from American shores.

Above: *A captured German submarine gets under way with a United States crew aboard.*

Below: *Four survivors from a German submarine crew float alongside a Coast Guard rescue plane.*

Members of the crew on the U.S. Coast Guard cutter
Spencer *run for their battle stations. (Chapter 11)*

Left above: *Captain Paul R. Heineman* (left), *escort commander in the North Atlantic, talks to Commander Harold S. Berdine* (right), *skipper of the* Spencer.

Left below: *A merchant tanker refuels two escort ships while steaming along at sea, a technique which Captain Heineman helped develop.*

Above: *A torpedoed United States tanker sends columns of black, oily smoke billowing into the air.*

Below: *British and Polish destroyers go to the assistance of an Allied convoy bound for a Russian port.*

As the Liberty ship John Finch, *built and launched within 24 days, floats out into the basin, a gigantic crane swings a keel for another new ship into position.*

Anti-aircraft cannon go into action aboard the British
Duke of York, which helped destroy the German bat-
tleship Scharnhorst. *(Chapter 16)*

Shipyards such as the one above, photographed in 1941,
were responsible for making the United States mer-
chant fleet the largest in the world.

A radar operator aboard the USS Augusta *is moving the dials to get a sharper image on the round scope.*

A convoy as seen from aboard a United States warship.

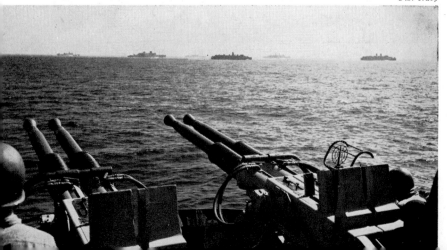

A spud pierhead is towed across the English Channel to be used in one of the prefabricated harbors set up on the Normandy Coast during the invasion.

in arriving, and would tell them exactly what cargoes they were carrying—so expert were the German spies on shore. Most of the U-boat commanders gave the crews of merchantmen a chance to get away in rafts before opening fire, although some were known to machine-gun sailors in the water.

Sometimes the submarines used tricks to get their victims. One torpedoed a Canadian corvette out in front of a convoy. After she had sunk, the U-boat sent out a radio message, pretending that it was from the radio operator of the corvette and asking for the convoy's position. When this was given, the submarine sailed straight to the convoy and torpedoed several other ships. On another occasion, a U-boat waited in the path of an American merchant ship at night and sent a blinker message: "This is the lightship. You are going on the rocks. Change course and pass close to my position." When the unsuspecting vessel did so, she was torpedoed and twenty men were killed.

As the months went on, the U-boats' score rose. In March, 1942, twenty ships were sunk in one week. On the last day of that month, six ships went down in twenty-four hours. In the Gulf Sea Frontier there were more sinkings in May than there were in any area in any month up to that time: forty-one ships destroyed by only half a dozen submarines. In the Caribbean U-boats felt so sure of themselves that one shelled an oil refinery on the shore, and another sailed right into the harbor at St. Lucia and torpedoed two ships docked there.

By midsummer, over 360 ships—a total of about two and a quarter million gross tons—had been lost to America. (The sinkings of merchant ships are generally expressed in gross tons, which refers to the entire internal cubic capacity of the ship in tons of 100 cubic feet each.) Some had been hit within full view of carefree vacationers on the beaches. "Papa" Doenitz reported smugly, "Our submarines are operating close inshore along the coast of the United States, so that bathers and sometimes entire coastal cities are witnesses to that drama of war . . ."

And in exchange, America had destroyed eight submarines. At the rate Germany was producing them, these could be replaced in two weeks.

10

Striking Back

America was like a boxer, groggy from the first punishing attack, but rallying. First he studies his opponent, then he uses science and skill, then he gathers his strength and goes in for the final knockout.

The first step was taken in March, 1942, when the Atlantic Fleet Antisubmarine Warfare Unit was organized. Its job was primarily study: the collection of information about submarine attacks and the analyzing of escort methods of defense. Second, it was responsible for training teachers who would in turn be able to run schools of instruction on how to fight the U-boats.

Working closely with this outfit was an organization called *Asworg*—the Antisubmarine Warfare Operations Research Group. Hitler was suspicious of scientists and forced some of the best ones to flee from Germany. Many others were drafted into the army. But in *Asworg,* as in its British counterparts, America and England used their scientists to the utmost and drew from them many weapons and studies in the use of weapons which did much to bring victory.

Three of the most important weapons were sonar (which the British called asdic), radar, and "huff-duff." Without them, not all the courage in the world would have helped against the U-boats.

Sonar was short for "sound-navigation ranging." In effect, this apparatus sent out a sound too high to be heard. This sound, traveling through the water, bounced off the hull of a submarine, returning an echo in the form of a high-pitched *ping*. The *ping* was heard at various degrees of pitch, lower or higher, depending on the kind of target it bounced from and the movements of the target. These changes in pitch, known as the Doppler effect, together with the time taken for the echo to return, allowed a trained sonar operator to tell a submarine from other objects under the sea, and to calculate its bearing, course, and speed. Sonar was carried in a compartment on a ship's bottom and its steady rapid note was the accompaniment to every voyage.

As sonar was the ears of a ship, radar was its eyes. Radar apparatus acts in much the same way as sonar, but instead of a sound it sends out radio waves which bounce back and register as pips of light on a screen. Radar could not be used under water; its chief use was to find submarines on the surface, particularly at night when they tried to creep in under cover of darkness.

"Huff-duff," the high-frequency direction finder, picked up the radio messages of U-boats at sea. When a number of huff-duff stations were receiving, they could get cross-bearings on a U-boat that was sending by radio and so fix its position. By checking constantly on these bearings, shore stations could plot the courses of submarines and relay these courses to convoys so that the escort ships would know where the enemy was, or estimate where he would be.

Many other weapons, or variations on these basic weapons, were developed as the war continued. A valuable one was a powerful searchlight for aircraft. Another was a special microwave radar that could be mounted on patrol planes. The German search receivers could not pick up this type of radar nor could the enemy ever figure out a way to jam or dodge it, so that it became one of the best submarine finders the Allies had.

For the actual job of killing submarines, the primary weapon was the depth charge. This was a bomb thrown over the side of a ship and set to explode at different depths. The commonest looked much like metal barrels, and were called "ashcans." They were fired from special projectors called Y-guns or K-guns because of their resemblance to those letters. Using depth charges meant a certain amount of guesswork, since there was never any way of figuring out exactly how far down a submarine had dived. To be of any use the depth charge had to explode close to the submarine's hull, but sonar would not work when a ship was right over a submarine because the noise of the propellers blanketed its echoes. For these reasons, it was necessary to drop a pattern of depth charges, and to try to outguess the U-boat commander. Such battles resembled duels between two blind men in a football stadium.

Weapons alone were not enough. The United States began a program of shipbuilding. Many new cargo ships were turned out—we shall come to these later—and for the navy quantities of patrol craft, cutters, subchasers, and especially destroyers were ordered. Shipyards went on a twenty-four-hour schedule; workmen and their employers alike gave up time and money to get the ships built.

In the first months of the attack on the United States coast, we were taken completely by surprise and consequently there were not enough escort vessels to cover the coastal lanes. Convoys require escort ships; without protection, a convoy is just a larger target than a single ship. So a system of short runs was started, called the "bucket brigade" by Admiral Andrews, the commander of the Eastern Sea Frontier. By this system, merchant ships sailed as close to the shore as they could during the day, going about 120 miles at a jump. At night they put in at protected anchorages to rest.

To help in the job of guarding the coast, a number of civilians volunteered their services. Many who owned small boats were formed into the Coastal Picket Patrol—more often called the "Hooligan Navy." Many more who owned and operated their own airplanes were organized into the Civil Air Patrol. In all sorts of weather, they maintained a steady watch on the sea, reporting suspicious objects and sometimes finding survivors of torpedoings whom the larger, faster planes had missed.

By May of 1942, the navy was able to establish regular convoys protected by fighting ships and given increased air cover. Airplanes were especially important in this work. Not only could they patrol, find and rescue shipwrecked seamen, and report the positions of submarines to escort vessels, but they were also very effective as U-boat killers—so much so that even the appearance of an unarmed scout plane was often enough to make a submarine dive. Navy planes based at Argentia, Newfoundland, sank the first two submarines which fell victim to the United States Navy in the Atlantic; the third and fourth were downed by ships; the fifth kill was made by a Bermuda-based plane. All told, planes accounted for eight U-boats in 1942.

The combination of protected convoys and good air cover had an immediate effect. Between

January and June of 1942 one hundred merchant ships had been sunk in the Eastern Sea
Frontier alone, but in July only three went
down, and for the rest of the year—none.

Unfortunately, however, the U-boats had not
been wiped out, as some Americans supposed.
They had simply moved into more profitable
waters. The PQ convoys, the name given to
those which ran between Iceland and North
Russia, were attacked again and again, and late
in the summer the Caribbean and the South
Atlantic were bitter battlegrounds.

The greatest problem, for Americans at least,
was to learn the methods of escorting a convoy.
The British had had two years of experience
and did their best to act as instructors, but in
war the best lessons are the most painful ones.
Just as a soldier learns to keep his head down
only by being under fire, so escort commanders
learned the techniques of fighting U-boats by
actually fighting them.

At first there were many mistakes. Escort

ships patrolled too close to the convoys, and so did not make contact with submarines early enough to keep them away. There was a tendency to use only a few depth charges instead of dropping large patterns. After firing off no more than half a dozen "ashcans," a ship would hurry to rejoin a convoy, leaving behind a completely unharmed U-boat, ready to attack again. Sometimes the merchantmen were too careless: in Convoy SC-118, for example, the three port columns failed to hear a whistle signal for an emergency turn, and as a result the convoy was split into two sections about fifteen miles apart.

By degrees, however, America learned. Each report that came in was carefully evaluated and criticized, and the lessons from it were distributed to the fleet. Training was tightened, and the scientists of *Asworg,* by collecting and studying data, were able to contribute many practical details such as patterns of search for U-boats, types of patrols, and methods of countering new German inventions.

What the United States needed most were experienced commanders like Captain Walker, who were more interested in attack than defense, who wanted to destroy the submarines, not merely hold them off. Very soon such men emerged. One of them was Paul R. Heineman.

11

Heineman's Harriers

When Paul Heineman, a bronzed, blue-eyed, forceful officer reported for duty as escort commander in the North Atlantic, a month after the United States entered the war, he was given a set of instructions which showed the grim nature of the Atlantic battle. "Your job is to get the convoys through," said Admiral Bristol, the task force commander. "You are the boss out there.

We can't tell you what to do in each event, from the beach. You must use your best judgment as emergencies develop. *Whatever you do is right!*"

They were the best instructions Captain Heineman could have had. All through that year, the U-boats constantly changed their tactics. "They were like a football team," Heineman said, later. "They would go around the ends on one play and then through the line on the next." As soon as the escorts found ways of meeting their attacks, the U-boats would switch their methods, sometimes coming up on the flanks at night, sometimes drifting down on a convoy from ahead, attacking in pairs or by packs.

The new escort commander found himself without enough fighting ships to guard his convoys. Most of his ships were corvettes, unable to make enough speed or to search properly in heavy weather. It was hard for him to develop teamwork since the ships under his command were constantly changing, some being overhauled, others being shifted to other duties.

Some of the skippers hadn't enough training in antisubmarine warfare. But Heineman had spent twenty-five years in naval service. He jumped into the work with zest and, remembering what the Admiral had told him, used his best judgment to see the job through.

One of the worst problems he had to deal with was the fact that most of his escort vessels were "short-legged." That is, they could not carry enough fuel for all the steaming necessary to fight submarines and still get all the way across the ocean. In the beginning, escorts frequently dropped out and ran home for lack of fuel; on one convoy, for instance, the escort group was reduced from seven to four ships for just this reason.

Heineman was the first escort commander to overcome this handicap by developing the trick of refueling his escort ships from merchant tankers while steaming along at sea. He had adapters made for the tankers' fuel-oil deck fittings and stocked his ships with plenty of hose used for washing decks. When a ship needed fuel it would be brought alongside a tanker and the hose and adapters passed over to the merchant ship. The hose would be hooked up to the tanker's deck connection, and oil could then be pumped over to the fighting ship's open tank. Using this method—the "alongside method" of fueling—escorts were able to get precious oil in practically all conditions of weather and sea without the convoy's having to change its course or speed. From then on, the escorts had no excuse for breaking off early, but could remain with the group until the end of the voyage.

In the fall of 1942, Heineman was summoned to a conference with the British Admiral, Max Horton, commander in chief of the Western Approaches, and asked to explain his system in detail. When Heineman had finished, Admiral "Max" said, "If the Americans can do it, we can do it!" and at once gave orders for hose, adapters, and at least four tankers to be so equipped for each convoy. From then on, not only Heineman's unit but all the merchant convoy units in the North Atlantic used this method.

Although Heineman's unit changed often, he did have several "Treasury" class cutters, two of which, *Spencer* and *Campbell,* he used as escort flagships. There were also four more or less permanent corvettes, the British *Dianthus* and the Canadian *Rosthern, Trillium,* and *Chilliwack.* With these plucky little ships he forged a team that fought through one of the bitterest winters in the North Atlantic. "Heineman's Harriers" was the name given to them by the task force commander, and this nickname was soon known throughout the northern ocean.

They achieved a reputation for dash and courage, and also for their unorthodox ways of getting things done. On one trip, for instance, one of the merchant ships broke the strict rule about keeping lights out. Heineman had tried to get the convoy commodore to discipline the violators of security, but night after night their lights showed. He sent the *Rosthern* to scold the ship through a bull-horn, but without success. Finally, *Rosthern*'s skipper opened fire with a fifty caliber machine gun, and tapped the iron hull of the merchant ship gently with a couple of dozen rounds. The lights went out. From then on, this method was used as standard procedure.

In the course of two dozen convoys, Heineman guided and watched his officers, worked at training them, and spent endless hours on the bridge of his flagship while the convoys crashed through snow, icy rain, high winds, and heavy seas. In that long year he saw himself and his skippers change from uncertain men who sometimes fumbled badly, to a smoothly operating and quick-thinking group which killed the enemy and brought the convoys to port.

February and March, 1943, were the months of greatest strain. On February 12th, Escort Unit A-3, as the group was then called, took over the 63 merchant ships of Convoy ON-166. The first nine days were comparatively quiet—except for a storm that lasted seventy-two hours—but on the twenty-first the wolf packs struck. For the next four days more than twenty submarines snapped at the convoy in one attack after another. There were only seven escorts yet they managed to keep the U-boats at a distance all the first day, losing two of their merchant flock but sinking one of the submarines.

On the evening of the second day they were attacked by U-606, which had been trailing them. It rose and torpedoed three ships on the convoy's left flank. A Polish corvette, *Burza,* came racing up to join the escort and depth-charged the sub. It dived, but had to come quickly back to the surface since its pressure hull was cracked. The *Campbell,* astern of the convoy, set course to ram, and as the two ships crashed together the submarine's hydroplanes hit the *Campbell* and tore a hole in her hull. Firing with every gun, the *Campbell* forced the Germans to abandon ship, and the submarine went to the bottom.

Altogether, before this hard four-day battle was over, seven merchant ships had been sunk in exchange for two subs. The weather was too rough for the ships to refuel at sea, and the *Dianthus* used every drop of oil aboard to get to port—paint-mixing oil, mineral oil, and even gunnery oil—finally coasting into harbor with every tank bone-dry.

Only twenty-four hours after they had landed Heineman's team were sent out again with Convoy SC-121. Weary as they were, they had to fight off one wolf pack after another. Since they had had so little time in port, the strain showed in their gear: half the ships' radars didn't work, the *Dauphin's* steering apparatus broke down, and the flagship's communications system failed during one attack. Nevertheless, they brought all but seven of the convoy through, a heroic feat in the face of all the odds.

The Harriers got their next submarine in April, with Convoy HX-233. This time Heineman was in the *Spencer* when they made sound contact with U-175, approaching the convoy from ahead. *Spencer* kept the sub down with two depth-charge attacks. Then, steaming between the columns of the convoy, she kept contact with the U-boat and continued the attack with depth charges. Once the U-175 was clear of the convoy, the *Spencer* coached in the *Duane*.

When the submarine surfaced, the two cutters began firing at it. Their fire was so heavy and so accurate that the U-boat began to sink. Its commander was killed and his crew surrendered. This kind of action was possible because the Harriers had become so skillful and so disciplined. A year earlier, no escort commander would have dared to follow a submarine between the columns of a convoy, and few would have been able to keep sound contact in spite of the explosions and the various propeller noises.

Captain Heineman's experience and knowledge were valuable to all escort leaders, so in May, 1943, he was made commanding officer of the Antisubmarine Warfare Unit of the Atlantic Fleet. In this job he had three major objectives. In the first place, he had seen clearly that the biggest problem was the lack of a standard method of fighting submarines. There were at least four different methods, each taught in a different school of antisubmarine warfare. So to begin with, he pushed for a standard doctrine of attack. He carried out an intensive course of training for specialists in antisubmarine warfare and then saw to it that these trained officers were sent to ships to put their training to best use.

The work of Captain Heineman, and of other brave officers like him, showed in the changing course of the struggle in the Atlantic. He himself was on duty in the Pacific at the time the war ended, and to the three Legion of Merit medals he had won for his work against the submarines in the Atlantic, a fourth was added for action against the Japanese while in command of the cruiser *Biloxi*.

Many years later, when he had been retired from the navy with the rank of rear admiral, Heineman wrote of the Atlantic battle: "It was an almost continuous job of plugging along, begging for ships, equipment, and air cover, training while in port, and begging for decent convoy discipline. But the thing that got us all through the job was the all-important will to win.''

It was this spirit which was to make all the difference between defeat and victory at the moment of crisis.

12

The Bad Year

In the battle for the Atlantic, the year 1942 was outstanding. It was the worst of the war.

During the first half of the year, the U-boats had their picnic along the American coast. Not only were many lives lost, as well as thousands of tons of fuel oil and shipping and supplies, but the whole schedule of shipments to England and Russia was in danger. In the Atlantic, the

Allies lost over three million tons of shipping altogether—568 ships—at a cost to the enemy of only 14 submarines.

Admiral Doenitz's boys had the whole ocean to romp in. As soon as countermeasures were put into effect in one area, Doenitz would move his submarines to another front and take the Allies off guard there. In July he sent some U-boats into the Caribbean Sea where in three months they sank seventy-five ships, most of them under the very noses of their escorts. Then they turned their attention to the South Atlantic and sank five big homeward-bound ships, including the great liner *Laconia*. The latter part of the year saw a renewed attack on the North Atlantic lanes. Here, the lack of very long range aircraft was one of the Allies' headaches, for it meant there was a gap in mid-ocean where there could be no air cover, and the wolf packs took advantage of this. In August more than a hundred ships were sent to the bottom. November saw the heaviest losses of the whole war: 117

ships in that month alone were blasted by U-boats.

In spite of the heavy losses, it was hard for the Allies to strike back. The great invasion of North Africa by Allied armies was under way. Warships had to be concentrated in the Mediterranean to guard supply lines and troop convoys, so that even fewer escorts were left to guard the Atlantic routes. And in the Pacific, things looked black: Java and Burma had been lost to the Japanese, and the Australians were fearful of being attacked. It was necessary to divert some warships to the Pacific to protect the supply and troop convoys going to the East.

"The U-boat attack," said Mr. Churchill, "was our worst evil. It would have been wise for the Germans to stake all upon it."

Fortunately, Hitler guessed wrong again. He was certain that the Allies planned to invade Norway, which he called "the zone of destiny in this war." Therefore, he drew away submarines and surface ships from other areas and concentrated them around Norway. This did not disturb the overall plans of the Allies. But it did have one bad effect on convoys. Among the surface ships was the giant battleship *Tirpitz,* largest in the world at that time. *Tirpitz* was held ready at Trondheim, a deep fjord on the Norwegian coast from which she could steam out to assault any convoys on the roads between England, Iceland, and North Russia. The presence of this great ship in those waters was a constant menace. It meant that the Allies had to keep a number of battleships ready to meet her, since the smaller escort vessels would have no more effect on the *Tirpitz* than a gang of boys with BB guns. Warships which could have been used to good advantage in other places were held within the limits of the northern waters. But on the other hand, the *Tirpitz* —and several other heavy, but smaller, German ships—were also held there instead of being out in the Atlantic where they could smash the more important convoys from America and Canada to England.

As it was, plenty of damage was done to the Russian convoys, and this had a serious effect on the whole war.

During the first months of 1942, the Russians had stalled the German blitz and forced the Nazis back on several fronts. The bitter Russian winter helped the Allied side, too. With the coming of spring, the Germans planned another push, toward the oil region of the Caucasus and also north against the city of Leningrad, the capital of Russia. By attacking before the Germans were ready, the Russians gained time. But the invaders were still powerful. It became more and more important to send ammunition, trucks, planes, and guns to the hard-fighting Russians.

In June, Convoy PQ-17 sailed from Iceland. (The letters PQ were assigned to Russian-bound convoys.) There were thirty-four merchantmen, guarded by six destroyers, four corvettes, two anti-aircraft ships, two submarines, and seven other small ships. In addition, there were three rescue ships whose job was to save men from the water, and there was a fleet oiler, for by now the technique of refueling at sea had been developed. The escort was supported by two British and two American cruisers, three destroyers, and, scattered along the Norwegian coast, nine British and two Russian submarines as advance scouts.

The size of the escorts and supporting force shows not only how important this convoy was but also how great was the danger from German ships that might attack from their bases in Norway. For in addition to the *Tirpitz* there were the battle cruiser *Hipper*, pocket battleships *Luetzow* and *Scheer*, and about twelve destroyers. There was also a swarm of submarines and planes.

PQ-17 was bound for the Russian port of Archangel. On the first of July, steaming through heavy patches of fog and ice floes, the convoy was sighted by the enemy. The first attacks came from torpedo planes, but these were driven off. The next day more planes came in as well as some U-boats. The destroyers took care of the submarines, and heavy anti-aircraft fire brought down one plane. There were more planes—twenty-six of them—on the following day. Then came the fireworks of the Fourth of July.

At three in the morning, a plane zoomed out of the fog and torpedoed an American ship. With her engine room out of commission, the ship had to be abandoned. A few hours later, over a glassy sea, bombers and torpedo planes poured in. The escort fought back and knocked three of them out of the sky. The Naval Armed Guard on one of the merchant ships opened up two tanks that were being carried on deck, broke ammunition out of the cargo in the hold, and opened fire with the tanks' guns. They disabled another plane.

Late in the day still another flight of planes came over and hit four ships. The escorts put up a bitter fight, and one destroyer, U.S.S. *Wainwright,* in spite of heavy strafing, kept many of the planes away by her accurate long-range anti-aircraft fire. Several times she dodged torpedoes, missing them by a hair, but she damaged three or four of the enemy and broke up two attacks.

All day long the battle continued. At nine that night, a signal went to the commander of the escort force: "Withdraw to the westward at high speed." It was believed that the *Tirpitz* and her supporting ships were sailing to cut off the convoy. If this were so, the escort was no match for the battleships. All that could be done was to save it for future fighting. As for the convoy, its only chance was to disperse. A second signal came half an hour later: "Convoy is to scatter."

There were 450 miles to go before reaching port. It was every ship for herself. For two frightful weeks the wolves and vultures, U-boats and planes, pulled down one vessel after another, or caught little groups and ripped them to shreds.

Some of them, hugging the ice, were bombed and sunk. Their crews died in the biting sea, or froze to death in open lifeboats. Some were picked up by other ships, only to be torpedoed again by U-boats and drowned. Some of the survivors were rescued by Russian vessels, others were picked up by escorts, and one group was given shelter by a camp of Russian children.

Some of the ships fought back, although they were armed with nothing but .30-caliber machine guns, or 3-inch guns. Even so, they accounted for some of the enemy dive bombers.

One little group that came through unharmed consisted of six merchant ships and an armed trawler. The master of one of the ships, George Salvesen, was a veteran arctic sailor. He suggested to the others that they paint the starboard sides of their ships white, and cover the hatches with white tablecloths and sheets. After doing this, they broke their way through the ice as far as they could go, turned their white sides to the sea and sat tight. Although enemy planes were all around, none spotted them through the camouflage and eventually all seven got safely to Archangel.

Of the thirty-three cargo ships which had left

Iceland, twenty-two were sunk, as well as the fleet oiler and one of the rescue ships. Only 70,000 out of almost 200,000 tons of the desperately needed supplies reached the Russians.

The irony of it was that the *Tirpitz* had done all this damage without ever coming near the convoy. She had done her part simply by existing. The threat of her coming had been enough to break up the convoy, and the individual ships were then helpless victims for the planes and U-boats.

13

Bomb Alley

The fate of Convoy PQ-17 did not stop the flow of supplies to Russia. Much was still going through the Persian Gulf and across the Pacific. But it was felt to be wiser to hold up the arctic convoys until winter, when the long night began.

The Russians, however, pressed urgently for supplies, saying that they were holding the

Germans on three fronts and needed the extra help. They said they felt the other Allies were not doing their share. But Britain was fighting hard in Africa and in the East, and she had also to bear the main burden of escorting the northern convoys. There were some sharp notes exchanged between the heads of the two countries. In the end, it was decided to send another convoy in September. PQ-18 was accordingly made up, and steamed out on the second of that month.

In the minds of most sailors, the arctic convoys at the edge of the ice pack, 900 miles from the North Pole, were the worst on any sea. "Bomb Alley" was the name they gave to that route, and it was one of the few places of action in the war where men prayed for bad weather.

Heavy snow or fog meant that the German planes could not find the ships, or would be grounded. On the other hand, bad weather had its own drawbacks. The heavy seas froze as they crashed on the decks, and there were long white

Convoys to the U.S.S.R.

beards of ice on the railings. Ice coated the guns, and spray frosted the men's faces. In summer there was no sheltering darkness; in winter there was endless gloom and even colder weather. A man in the sea had small chance of living long enough to be picked up. When the ships landed at Murmansk, there was nothing for the seamen to do. Even though the Russians tried to be friendly there was no entertainment, very little food, and not even safety because German planes from a base only thirty-five miles away came over in waves every day to blast the waterfront.

Bomb Alley lived up to its name with convoy PQ-18. Forty merchantmen set out, and this time the Admiralty sent every available fighting ship with the convoy, almost one to each merchantman. In addition to twenty-one destroyers, four corvettes, and some smaller vessels, there were an anti-aircraft cruiser and, for the first time, an escort carrier, *Avenger,* with fifteen Hurricane fighters aboard.

On the twelfth of September, the convoy was marked down by a Nazi patrol plane. The next day, bombers and torpedo planes began coming over, "so thick," as one seaman reported, "that they looked like a swarm of bees." Some were painted black with orange wing tips; a navy officer said that they were "weird and awful to behold."

At once, the escort began to put up a very heavy anti-aircraft barrage, which was so accurate that it took the enemy by surprise. The sky was crisscrossed with tracers, the sea boiled with explosions. For the next nine days the battle went on.

On one ship a powerful seaman carried two-hundred-pound ammunition boxes from the lazarette to the guns by himself, so that the guns kept firing and splashed four planes. On another ship, in spite of heavy attack, the crew stuck to their gun until they were blown away from it by an explosion. A Naval Armed Guard commander noted, "I have not slept longer than two hours at night for the past three nights. My food is brought to the bridge. I do not even leave to visit the head. And so it went with the majority of the ship's crew. . . . It was 21 hours' duty out of every 24, if one wanted to live."

There were submarine attacks as well, but fortunately the enemy's surface ships never came out. In this almost endless battle the *Avenger*'s planes showed the importance of aircraft carrier support, for on the fourteenth they flew up to intercept the enemy aircraft and operated so well that the four attacks from the air on that day sank only a single ship. On the fifteenth another raid by seventy bombers was fought off by the Hurricanes from the *Avenger,* and the attack failed completely. The planes also served to spot U-boats and to guide destroyers to them.

On the evening of the sixteenth, the larger escort ships had to join a southbound convoy, leaving PQ-18 with an escort of about ten ships. However, the next day four Russian destroyers joined the convoy, and by now the Germans had become more cautious. In most cases they flew in at high level to escape the anti-aircraft fire and dropped their bombs and torpedoes before they were close enough to be sure of a hit. Still, they continued their raids right up to the day the convoy entered port.

Twenty-seven of the forty ships reached Archangel. They had come through the worst air attack of this route. On some days more than a hundred torpedo planes and a hundred bombers had been counted in the skies. But the enemy paid with four planes for every ship they sank and, in addition, three submarines lost.

The grim struggle began to turn in the Allies' favor. After the terrible punishment endured by PQ-18, the Allies sent nothing but a small number of unescorted ships to Russia until December. Then the convoys were begun again, this time with new code letters: JW instead of PQ for outward bound groups.

JW-51A had a "tourist cruise"; not a single enemy plane was seen. Its second section, JW-51B, met a hunting pack of German surface ships: *Luetzow, Hipper,* and six destroyers. After a confused fight in semidarkness and snow squalls, the British escorts sank one of the destroyers and beat off the attack. Although one escort ship was lost, all the merchant ships of the convoy came safely through.

Two more JW convoys were run in 1943 before the long daylight began again. Neither lost a ship. The balance had definitely tipped.

By spring the Germans were cleaned out of Tunisia, in North Africa, and the Mediterranean was safe enough so that the supply route from England, past Gibraltar, through the Suez Canal, and along the Persian Gulf to Russia could be used during the summer. By the end of 1943, the arctic route had become comparatively safe.

The JW convoys had one more important effect. After the successful voyage of convoy JW-51B, Hitler definitely decided against building any more capital ships. He had never been very enthusiastic about the navy. Admiral Raeder, who had always wanted big ships and had demanded a fleet air arm, was now forced to resign. His place was taken by the U-boat champion, Doenitz. This marked the end of the

German high seas fleet. Submarines, although deadly, could not carry on a naval war. They could sink ships, but they could not defeat a navy. And as the Allies built more and better antisubmarine vessels, and learned how to strike back at the U-boats, the effectiveness of the underwater enemy was weakened.

From this moment on, therefore, the Germans were fighting on the defensive. They could no longer hope to win the battle for the Atlantic supply lines. They could only hope to prolong the war and delay the moment of Allied victory.

14

Ships

By the time that dark year, 1942, drew to an end, about eight million tons of shipping had been sunk. The U-boats had been accounting for ships faster than the Allies could build them. "Shipping," said Winston Churchill, "was at once the stranglehold and the sole foundation of our war strategy." Ships and more ships were needed—not only escorts to find and smash the enemy, but also cargo ships, tankers, and troop ships to pour men and supplies and oil into the crucial battles of the coming years.

Two months after the United States entered the war, a new agency was formed. This was the War Shipping Administration, headed by Rear Admiral Emory Scott Land, a short, peppery man with the temperament of a tornado. He was also head of the Maritime Commission, and his job was to replace the twenty thousand tons of shipping lost every day, and then to double the replacements. Many people disliked Admiral Land, who certainly stepped on lots of toes, spoke out at the top of his voice, and never soft-pedaled what he had to say. But in the end, the job was done.

It was not done by Land alone, although he led the way. The work of the shipbuilders of America was called "one of the mightiest of the many miracles of production in the war effort."

Every existing shipyard was crammed with hulls under construction. New shipyards—eighteen of them—were built and managed by the

Maritime Commission. It took too long to construct the standard types of cargo vessels so a new type of ship was designed, a ship that soon symbolized the whole hard grind of the Atlantic battle. This was the Liberty ship.

When President Roosevelt first saw the plans for the Liberty, he chuckled and called it an ugly duckling. Many members of the Maritime Commission and other government bureaus warned Admiral Land that it was a waste of good money to build these ships, for they would be slow, ugly, cramped, and expensive. He was heading for trouble, they warned. "See you in jail," growled Land, and went right ahead.

The first Liberty, the *Patrick Henry,* was delivered at the end of December, 1941. From that time until the war's end, twenty-seven hundred Ugly Ducklings proved their value by carrying more than seventy-five percent of the United States' cargo overseas. It was true they were slow, making only 11 knots as against the 15½ and 17 knots of the two other principal cargo types, the C2 and C3. They were uncomfortable, with small cabins and tangles of exposed pipes in awkward places. But they were easy to build, even by the thousands of people who had never worked in a shipyard before. They could be prefabricated: that is, standard parts such as masts, booms, winches, and funnels, and shaped steel slabs could be made in different factories and then quickly assembled in the yards. The engines were simple to operate, and so were the loading booms and all the other parts.

When they were ready for sea, these lumbering crates could be manned even by inexperienced sailors. Equally important, they could carry 10,800 tons of cargo, which was more than the C2 could carry and not much less than the C3, although the Liberty was smaller than either of these general cargo ships. And there was room, too, for plenty of guns for defense.

The Liberty ships were typical of the spirit of America at war. To build them, men who had never been on a ship, women who had never seen a welding torch before, even teen-agers, worked long hard hours. Young men who had never sailed in any other kind of ship manned the guns and fought their way through heavy seas. Some of the ships were named for famous Americans such as John Adams, others for Americans who had never been heard of before —seamen like Carl Webb who went down with their ships.

They were assembly-line ships, so much alike that a sailor coming back to the docks in the blackout might stumble on board what looked like a familiar ship, make his way along familiar companionways, and go to a familiar cabin only to find in the morning that he was on the wrong ship.

Shipyards competed against each other to cut down the time it took to turn out a ship. In the month of December, 1942, more ships were built than in all of the year 1941. The first Liberty took 244 days to build; two years later, they were being built in about a month and a half. One shipyard owner, Henry J. Kaiser, tore into the field with almost no experience, and in less than a year had cut construction time from seventy-two days to forty-six days. His average was around five weeks, although on occasion he could turn out a ship in ten days.

At the same time, fighting ships were being built for the navy. These could not be rushed in quite the same way, nor could they be as simple as the cargo vessels. Precision was needed for speed and strength. It was not until late in 1943 that the navy began to get enough ships capable of dealing properly with the U-boat menace.

Among the most needed were subchasers and patrol craft, but best of all were the swift, strong, well-armed DEs, destroyers specially built for escort-of-convoy duty. These were designed by the navy to be mass-produced. Where a regular destroyer took nine months to build and cost seven million dollars, a DE could be launched in four months at half the cost.

Long and slender, the DEs were hard to hit with a torpedo. Armed with eight or nine depth-charge projectors, with three- or five-inch cannon, twenty-millimeter Oerlikon guns, and forty-millimeter Bofors, the DE was a match for any submarine.

Another new ship which was to play an important part in the battle, particularly in the Central Atlantic, was the CVE, a small aircraft carrier also designed specially for escort work. Converted from cargo-vessel hulls, the CVEs carried sixteen fighter planes and twelve torpedo bombers on their relatively short decks. Carriers like the *Bogue* and the *Card* soon made such reputations for themselves as U-boat killers that submarines, which for a while had tried fighting back at planes, tried wildly to escape as soon as they heard aircraft engines.

But in the last analysis, all the new ships depended on men to run them.

The navy had the job of training fighting men, specialists who could get the most out of the special antisubmarine ships. A unified training command was organized for the Atlantic, and under its wing Captain Paul Heineman commanded the Antisubmarine Warfare Unit, which set up new and better training schools. Instead of transferring officers around to different jobs, as the navy had always done, a new fraternity was formed of men with experience and skill in the particular art of fighting submarines. And from the schools in Miami and Rhode Island, and the Shakedown Task Force in Bermuda, came crews for the new escorts.

There were other men, however, who did not wear uniforms and who got little training. They didn't have ribbons or medals, and although they fought they weren't particularly known as fighting men. No one recognized them on the street. Yet without them, the battle for the Atlantic would have been lost.

15

And Men

A man in ragged clothes, wearing a pair of canvas sneakers that were torn and dirty, went into one store after another in New York City one afternoon. He wanted a pair of shoes. However, no one would sell them to him because he didn't have the necessary ration coupon. In some places, customers muttered, "Draft dodger!" or "slacker." In others, the clerks would not even wait on what appeared to be such a disreputable-looking tramp.

Appearances were deceiving. That man was a merchant seaman. His ship had been torpedoed and he had had to swim under flaming oil to escape. He had been one of a handful of survivors, sick, exhausted, and oil-soaked, pulled up from the freezing water by a rescue ship. He finally got his shoes by getting a slip from his draft board which allowed him to buy a pair. And as soon as he had them, he went down to the hiring hall of the National Maritime Union and got ready to go to sea again.

"Keep 'em Sailing!" was the slogan of the NMU, the union to which almost every ordinary seaman who sailed the Atlantic belonged. From the very beginning, this union, in spite of many disagreements with Admiral Land and with shipowners, set aside everything else in favor of winning the war. Its members made up the crews which manned the ships, hauling supplies from the United States to her allies.

Some of them were old-timers who had spent

all their lives at sea. Some of them were brand-new, young and green, like the boy on his first trip who saw the captain's parrot on the bridge and tried to catch it, thinking it was a bright-colored sea gull. The parrot growled, "What are you doing up here?" The young man turned red, saluted, and gulped, "Oh, excuse me, sir, I thought you were a bird."

All sorts of charges were made against the merchant seamen. It was said that many of them were "performers"—that is, that they were shiftless, drunk, and lazy. It was said that their pay was much higher than that of the regular navy sailor, and that most of them stayed in the merchant marine to escape being drafted and to get rich.

The union's answer to the first charge was to post the names of men who were known "performers" and to discipline them, or even keep them from sailing. To the second charge, the union replied that although merchant seamen did get higher pay than regular navy men, they had to pay for everything: their clothes, rubber suits, medical attention, board and keep, entertainment, the care of their families, and an income tax besides. There were no Post Exchanges for them, and no benefits.

The men of the merchant marine were a hard-boiled lot. They had to be. They might sail in a ship loaded with oil or TNT where a single lucky hit from a torpedo would give them no chance of survival. Their ships were often armed with nothing more than a couple of light machine guns. Some of the equipment was old and rusty; sometimes even the lifeboats were full of holes, or the old-fashioned cork life preservers would drown a man instead of keeping him afloat in the water. On some ships, Negro or Filipino seamen were not allowed to work. The NMU fought against these conditions for its members, asking that ships be better armed, inspecting equipment and urging that it be brought up to date, making many suggestions which shipowners and builders used. Along with the National Maritime Union were other sea unions, the Marine Firemen, Oilers and Wipers, the stewards' union, and the union of radio operators, all of whose members backed the war effort.

Little by little, things were worked out. Slowly, the restrictions against colored seamen were lifted. A few ships even had Negro officers, and at least two had Negro skippers. The merchant mariners, the shipowners, and the navy found ways of working out their disagreements together so that they could join in fighting the common enemy. The armaments—particularly anti-aircraft weapons—of the merchant ships were increased, and Naval Armed Guards were put aboard to work the guns and also to train gunners and assistants from among the crews. The Naval Armed Guard usually consisted of a young naval junior officer with a few blue-jackets. At first this meant additional disagreements, since the merchant seamen and the navy men didn't get on too well. But as time passed, and they all had to face the same dangers together, they came to admire each other. Soon, in the reports of Naval Armed Guard commanders, could be found words like those of Ensign Tritchler, aboard the *Alcoa Prospector:* "There has not been one instance of friction between the unlicensed merchant seamen and the men under my command. The courage and co-operation of all members of the ship's company . . . deserve the highest praise."

Navy men could be ordered to sail in dangerous waters. But the merchant seamen went voluntarily on trips from which hundreds never returned. No one could know whether a voyage would be completely uneventful, or disastrous.

Seventeen-year-old Walter Szarszen, on his very first trip, was reading in his bunk one night when a terrific explosion picked him up and threw him to the deck. It was a hot night and he had no clothes on, but he didn't even stop to grab a life preserver. His one thought was to get up to the boat deck as fast as possible. With other seamen he scrambled up the ladder. The alarm bells were ringing. All inside lights went out. Above, the deck was lighted by flames from burning oil, and the darkness was torn apart by the flashes of cannon. A submarine had torpedoed the ship on the starboard side, and was now firing at her with its deck guns.

Boats were lowered from the sinking ship. A shell from one of the U-boat's guns hit one boat and smashed it. "We cursed them plenty," Szarszen said later, "but at the same time everyone was pretty calm. I was embarrassed by being naked, even in the dark and confusion, so I borrowed a pair of pants from the second assistant engineer whose room was on the main deck, and I felt a little better even if they were too big for me. But a half an hour later, I lost them sliding down a cable to the one life raft that was left in the water. The cable was frayed and I tore my hands. I found myself several feet from the raft. I can't swim and I thought sure for a minute I wouldn't make it. When I did get aboard, I had to help row like the dickens to keep the raft away from the flaming patches of oil that would have roasted us alive. We were so close the heat seared our faces. We were

picked up about two hours later by a subchaser."
And then, with a grin on his brown face, he
added, "Sure I'm going to ship out again. All
of us are."

Scarcely a day passed without the sad tale
of survivors. Some seamen got to know life rafts
as well as they knew their ships. There was
Elliot Gurnee, sole survivor of eight men who
got to a raft; the others died, and he drifted for
twenty-four days before being rescued. When
his rations gave out, he caught a sea gull and
two fish and ate them raw. The record for lone-
liness was made by Poom Lim, steward of a
British freighter, who spent 133 days alone on
a raft and kept himself alive by fishing with a
bent nail and a wire spring from the inside
of a flashlight.

Typical of the experiences of many men was
the story told to a reporter from the NMU *Pilot,*
by Charles Heaton, after his ship had been
shelled by a U-boat. (Heaton and some others
got away in a lifeboat.)

"There was no motor, just sails," he said. "We

didn't make much headway. Only one fish was caught—a three-incher—and the man who caught it ate it raw. We caught crabs and ate them raw. One guy made a salad from seaweed and mineral oil. The first week, the men swam every day but we had to stop because of sharks. We had plenty of rain for drinking water. . . . The dye in the sail didn't hold, and the rainwater we caught in the sail was pink, so we called it Pink Lady. Breakfast was one ounce of Pink Lady, one graham cracker, two squares of chocolate. Lunch, the same. For supper we had a real treat: three ounces of Pink Lady, two squares of chocolate, two graham crackers, and a third of a can of pemmican with a dash of mineral oil."

There was little recognition for these men of the merchant service. The union awarded small lapel pins to those of its members who were torpedoed. The government instituted a Merchant Marine Distinguished Service Medal. The first such medal was awarded by President Roosevelt in October, 1942, to Edwin P.

Chaney, Jr., who, during an enemy attack, and in spite of severe burns, saved many of his shipmates from a sea covered with flaming oil.

But medals and recognition meant very little to most of the merchant seamen. "We had a job to do and we did it," said one of them, after a JW convoy through snowstorms, subzero cold, perpetual darkness, and six days of air attack. "Ship out again? Sure we will. Somebody's got to get the stuff across!"

16

The Turn of the Tide

All the hard work of brave and determined men and women, the ships, the supplies, and the sacrifices began to pay off in 1943. In that year came the turning point of the war. Though there were long months still ahead, it could be definitely seen that the Allies were now taking the initiative, while the enemy was driven more and more to defend himself.

In February the German attack on the key Russian city of Stalingrad collapsed. Ninety thousand prisoners were taken, twenty-one German divisions were smashed, and the German general von Paulus and his whole staff were taken prisoner. By October the battered Germans were retreating everywhere in Russia.

May saw the coming of victory in North Africa, too, and now the Allies began to press closer to home. In July, Sicily was invaded, and taken in thirty-eight days. Mussolini was deposed as Italy's leader, and by September the Italians had surrendered. The German armies in Italy fought on, desperate and alone.

At the same time, bombers roared out from England over Germany every day, and in the late summer Berlin got the first taste of the heavy air bombardment that London had been taking for three years.

In January of that fateful year, President Roosevelt and Prime Minister Churchill met at Casablanca. There it was decided that "defeat of the U-boat must remain a first charge on the resources of the United Nations." Later in the year an Atlantic Convoy Conference was held in Washington to pool all the Allied resources in the Atlantic. Many steps toward better organization of the war on the ocean were taken. The United States and Britain stopped thinking in terms of naval battles, or air battles over the sea, and began to think and plan as a single great team, in which both naval and air operations were part of the same battle.

A new short-wave radar apparatus was developed, and improved techniques of using air radar and sonar were put into use. A new type of streamlined depth charge was invented. The U-boat passage in the Bay of Biscay, through which the submarines entered and left their headquarters, was blasted, particularly by rockets fired from airplanes. For a while the enemy tried sending U-boats through in groups on the surface and shooting back at the planes. This did them little good, and soon they had to return to their earlier tactics of diving and running. Even so, in July thirty-seven submarines were sunk, nearly half of them in the waters of the Bay itself.

Month by month, the ship losses fell. In March, U-boats had sunk over 500,000 tons of shipping. By June this dropped to only slightly more than 20,000 tons. And in exchange, in those four months, the enemy had lost eighty-four U-boats. This was only one less than had been sunk all during the year 1942.

During the stormy autumn months, Germany struggled to recover its submarine strength. New torpedoes, code-named "Wrens," were produced; these were attracted to the sound of an escort ship's propellers. Even if they were aimed badly they homed in on the propellers and exploded under the ship's stern. Almost at once, the Allies retaliated with a device called "Foxer." This was a set of metal rods towed some distance behind a ship. It attracted the acoustic torpedoes and made them explode harmlessly.

By June, attacks in the North Atlantic had dwindled to nothing. The U-boats went off to the South Atlantic and the Indian Ocean where defenses were weaker but where there were also fewer targets. The combined air and sea defenses of the convoys were now so strong that for every attack the Germans made they suffered severe losses. In the last three months of the year the score showed which way the wind was blowing: twenty-four merchant ships lost, against forty-six U-boats killed, in the Atlantic alone.

On the day after Christmas, came the climax.

Convoys to Russia had been getting through without damage, each one pouring in supplies to help throw the Germans still farther back. During the first three weeks of December, fifty-two merchantmen made the trip safely. Bomb Alley was as quiet as a country lane.

Admiral Doenitz prepared to change this. He planned a surface raid, using the *Scharnhorst,* the only one of his big ships available since the others were being either repaired or overhauled. Reports came to him that a convoy was leaving for Murmansk, and in rough weather he ordered the *Scharnhorst,* with five destroyers, to chase it.

England had expected this move and was ready. Not one, but two convoys were due to pass each other near Bear Island in the north: JW-55B going to Murmansk, and JW-55A returning home empty. In addition to strong escorts, the convoys were covered by two support groups: Force 1 made up of three cruisers, *Norfolk, Belfast,* and *Sheffield;* and Force 2, the battleship *Duke of York* with a cruiser and two destroyers.

Admiral Sir Bruce Fraser, in the *Duke of York,* set the stage. Knowing that the Germans were probably after JW-55B, he ordered the convoy to change course. Vice-Admiral Burnett, with the three cruisers of Force 1, was closest, so he was sent to help the escort ships. Fraser himself, with Force 2, hurried to close in also, although he was 350 miles to the southwest.

Early in the morning, on the day after Christmas, the *Scharnhorst* was picked up on the radar of one of Admiral Burnett's cruisers. She was alone, for her destroyers had been sent out to look for the convoy, and by a combination of accidents these destroyers never did rejoin the battleship.

The three British cruisers opened fire. One lucky shot from the *Norfolk* put the German ship's main radar antenna out of business. The *Scharnhorst* steamed away, trying to work north around the cruisers. In the high seas and strong wind she was much faster than they were. Admiral Burnett lost contact.

At this point, he could have sent the escort destroyers to look for the German ship. But he guessed that the *Scharnhorst* was trying to reach the convoy. In any case, that was where his main responsibility lay, for each convoy that got through to Russia shortened the war by a month, at least. It was his duty to stay with the merchant ships. He therefore decided to rejoin the convoy and wait to see if the *Scharnhorst* would come to *him*.

As it happened, it was the right decision. For the *Scharnhorst* had received an order from Doenitz himself: "Attack and destroy the convoy to help your comrades in their fight on the Eastern Front."

At noon, Admiral Burnett's patience was rewarded. The cruiser *Norfolk,* the same ship which had helped track down the *Bismarck,* found the bright pip on her radar screen which was the *Scharnhorst* steaming straight for the convoy. At once, Burnett set out to intercept her, and as soon as the white bow wave of the enemy could be seen in the gloom—for the arctic midday was almost as dark as night—he opened fire.

For the next twenty minutes, a duel raged. The *Scharnhorst*'s big eleven-inch guns hit the *Norfolk,* and the British destroyers could not get close enough to fire their torpedoes. Then the German ship broke off the action once again, and turned south to run for home. What the German commander did not know was that in

THE BATTLE FOR THE ATLANTIC

the south a surprise Christmas present was rushing to cut him off—Admiral Fraser in the *Duke of York,* with the rest of Force 2.

Admiral Burnett kept contact, shadowing the *Scharnhorst* by radar and reporting her course to Admiral Fraser. The range closed. The unsuspecting Germans were looking forward to finishing their Christmas celebration at home. Suddenly the dark sea was brightly lighted by star shells and parachute flares. An instant later, the first salvo from the *Duke of York*'s guns straddled the Nazi ship.

The British were between the *Scharnhorst* and her base. The German ship turned eastward and tried to get away at high speed. She would fire a broadside, then turn east and run, then swerve southward and fire again. From the *Duke of York* she could barely be seen—only a long, silvery-gray shape from which burst the orange flashes of gunfire. Now and then green or reddish glows twinkled on her, indicating where the British shells were hitting.

Force 2's destroyers slowly crept in, trying to get near enough to deliver a torpedo attack. The splashes of shells rose on either side of the *Duke of York*. Her masts were pierced and her radar cables cut, but she kept up a steady fire, hitting the German ship again and again. Aboard the *Scharnhorst,* thick black smoke poured through the ship. Blood and freezing sea water swirled through the turrets, and there were fires in several places.

Her guns still roared. But her speed had been reduced just enough for the destroyers to inch up on her, two on each side. Closer they came, with great waves washing up over their torpedo tubes and soaking the crews, their engines laboring. And at last, at about 2,000 yards, they released their torpedoes.

Again and again they raced in under heavy fire. More destroyers came up and sent in their salvos. The *Scharnhorst* was invisible—all that could be seen of her was a dull glow in a dense cloud of smoke.

All at once there came the sullen thump of an explosion, a big one that shook many of the attacking ships. Then, silence.

When the cruiser *Belfast* went in to inspect, she found among the wreckage and the oil thirty-six survivors out of a crew of two thousand. The last great battle between surface ships on the Atlantic was ended.

17

Preparation for Overlord

The danger of surface ships attacking the northern convoys was finished. Germany had one capital ship left: the *Tirpitz*, which had been hidden in a deep fjord in Norway. But in September, 1943, three months before the sinking of the *Scharnhorst*, two midget submarines had slipped through the defenses of the fjord and planted mines which damaged the big battleship. No sooner was she repaired than aircraft from a carrier found her and pounded her with bombs. Once more, repairs were started, but the *Tirpitz*'s death sentence had been signed. Lancaster bombers, carrying a special type of heavy bomb, searched her out in September of 1944 and sank her. Before that, however, Germany had written off her usefulness as a seagoing fighting ship.

At about the same time, the *Hipper* and *Luetzow* collided with each other and were damaged. Neither ever went to sea again.

The U-boat war, too, was on its last legs. It was not yet over by any means; only a couple of months before the war's end, submarines tried one final assault close to the English coast. Even though the war was all but lost, Doenitz tried to do as much harm as he could.

In January, 1944, he said, "The day will come when I shall offer Churchill a first-rate submarine war. . . . We will smash Britain's supply line with a new submarine weapon."

The new weapon was the snorkel tube, which allowed U-boats to stay submerged for very long periods, and to recharge their batteries without coming to the surface. But it was too late. The end was almost in sight.

The construction of new merchant ships was now far above Allied losses. For every cargo ship that went down, two submarines were destroyed. American troops in increasing numbers were sent across to Africa and Italy, as well as to England, to train for the coming invasion of Europe. And the supply lines from America to England, from England to Russia, grew stronger every day.

The Allied escort units were now part of a tight-knit, well-trained organization. They had plenty of ships, airplanes, and carriers. Excellent teamwork between ships and planes blasted the submarines on and under the sea. In the Mediterranean, a new tactic was developed: the "swamp" operation. By this method, the Allied force kept U-boats under until their crews were worn out and had to surface; then they were blown to bits. Everywhere U-boat commanders continued to fight, but it was clear they were more interested in surviving or in doing damage than in winning the war.

The Germans were being pressed back all along the immense Russian front, and up the Italian boot. The time was ripe for the long-planned landing on the coast of Europe, to take back France and Belgium and strike directly at the guarded center of Hitler's empire.

"Overlord" was the name given to this gigantic project.

From the start, it had been clear to the Allies that the war could not be ended without an invasion of Europe. For a long time, the Russians had been pressing for a "Second Front," an offensive through France or Belgium. Both President Roosevelt and Prime Minister Churchill had had to soothe the impatient Russians. They both agreed with Marshal Stalin, the Soviet leader, that the invasion was necessary and that it would crush the Germans between two armies moving from east and west. But it was not something that could be jumped into hastily.

The enemy was still very strong. The entire coast of Europe bristled with gun emplacements, pillboxes, mines. To take and keep a foothold anywhere would mean serious losses of men. The thing could not be done until it had at least a better than even chance of success.

To begin with, half a million American troops had to cross the ocean to England, where they would train and prepare. Millions of tons of supplies had to go with them. An equal number of British troops had to be made ready. Then the assault troops—176,000 men with 20,000 vehicles and thousands of tons of supplies—had to be transported to the coast of France. Special landing craft had to be designed and built to carry men, tanks, guns, and trucks from the ships to the shore.

There was another problem: the problem of where to land. The Germans were ready to destroy any port where ships might dock, or landing craft unload. A stretch of beaches on the Normandy coast was chosen, therefore, which would add to the element of surprise. There were no natural harbors on this coast, so one of the most amazing engineering feats ever attempted was proposed—to build an artificial harbor.

To do this, enormous structures had to be constructed, floated across the Channel at the last moment, and set in the proper places. Some were breakwaters, long steel floats which would be fastened in a line to break the force of the waves and protect the docks. Others were caissons: concrete boxes the size of five-story buildings, which would be towed by tugboats into position, where their compartments would be flooded so that they would sink. They would act as moorings, or docks for supply ships. Steel roadways floating on pontoons were planned as part of the harbor, and twenty-seven American cargo ships—old ones, which were no longer seaworthy—were to be sunk to add to the break-water.

All the preparations, as well as the success of the final operation, rested on the defeat of the submarines in the Atlantic. When this had been accomplished, "Overlord" could begin.

18

The Battle's End

D-Day was set. It was to be June 6, 1944.

At five minutes past midnight, word came to Doenitz's headquarters that Allied paratroopers were landing in Normandy. This might be nothing but a raid, but the Admiral alerted two U-boat groups. The Germans knew that every port in England had been crowded with ships,

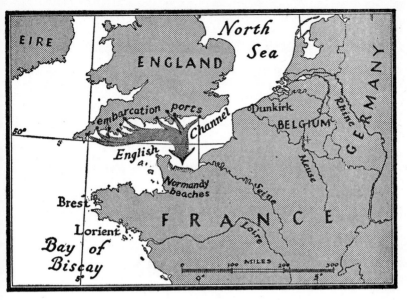

D-Day—the assault

and that strange objects like nothing that had ever been seen before were being built at docks in London and along the southern coast. But the secret had been well kept, even though the greatest amphibious operation in history was being planned.

At five in the morning, it became clear that it was not a raid but a full-fledged landing. German fliers saw Dunkirk in reverse—Dunkirk with a vengeance. The Channel was packed with ships, a vast armada of them, but this time they were going to France.

Doenitz ordered fifteen submarines, half of them equipped with snorkels, into the Channel. Another fourteen boats were thrown across the entrance to the Bay of Biscay. Motor torpedo boats and other light craft were sent out as well. It is possible that even at this point the Germans did not fully realize what was happening.

The Allies had taken all precautions against submarine attack. A screen of destroyers and torpedo boats guarded the Channel approaches, and three escort carriers stood ready near by. Furthermore, the air was literally black with a round-the-clock air patrol so that no U-boat could get through unseen.

All day long the transports wallowed in. The landing craft fought their way to the beaches through waves six feet high. Many were swamped; the rest came under fierce mortar and machine-gun fire. But they made their landings, and bloody struggles to secure the beaches began.

By nightfall the issue still hung in doubt. But after twenty-four hours the enemy had been driven back and the beachheads were firmly established. During that time no U-boat got close enough to a ship to deliver an attack. They kept trying. Five were sunk in the three days after D-Day, and seven were damaged. A week later they managed to sink two British frigates, and then toward the end of the month a corvette and an empty troopship. Four Liberty ships were torpedoed but were able to make port.

By early July, when the Germans were retreating, it could be seen that the U-boat attempt to stop the invasion had been a total failure. Thirteen submarines had been destroyed; the great invasion fleet had lost four ships. And two hundred vessels a day were making the crossing from England to France with supplies and reinforcements.

For the rest of the year, U-boats made scattered raids on convoys, but lost heavily for every ship they sank. During March and April, 1945, U-boats equipped with snorkels came close to the British coast where they hid on the sea bottom. Using their breathing tubes to stay under the surface, they were hard to find by sonar because of the confused echoes from rocks and wrecks. During these two months they succeeded in accounting for 130,000 tons of shipping. The end of the war was near, and yet they continued to torpedo cargo ships. It was as if, seeing the end, they wanted to drag as many men down to death with them as they could.

Submarines of a new type, faster and larger than any in use, were being built and Doenitz hoped that if he got enough of them he might yet manage to cut the Allied supply line. It would not bring him victory, but it would make the war last longer. However, materials were short and all sorts of unexpected "bugs" developed, so that luckily none of these boats saw action. The production of regular submarines went on, and sixty or seventy U-boats remained at sea, active to the last. Only a few days before the war ended, Doenitz said to his U-boat commanders, "We shall fight to the very last man. We shall never, never surrender."

On the eighth of May, 1945, this resolve turned to dust. On that day, Admiral Harold R. Burrough, R.N., acting for the Supreme Commander, ordered all U-boats at sea to surface and fly a black flag of surrender, to report their positions, and to proceed to the nearest port. Hitler was dead, and Doenitz, now leader of Germany, had surrendered to the Allies.

In many places, as from a fantastic game of hide-and-seek, the long wicked hulls rose up dripping, with black flags or dark blankets flying over their conning towers. Their crews were sullen and quiet. It was hard for them to believe that in spite of Doenitz's brave words the war was over.

Two U-boat commanders, staunch Nazis, refused to give up. They remained at sea, one of them still trying—although without success—to strike at convoys. At last they made their way to the Argentine where they hoped to hand their boats over to Nazi sympathizers. However, they were interned and their boats taken by the United States Navy.

On the afternoon of the twenty-eighth of May, both the United States Navy and the British Admiralty issued this statement:

"Effective at 2001 [8:01 P.M.] this date . . . no further trade convoys will be sailed. Merchant ships by night will burn navigation lights at full brilliancy and need not darken ship."

The long, hard battle was over at last. The seas were safe again.

Index

INDEX

INDEX

INDEX